Decorative Dressmaking

Sue Thompson

 Rodale Press, Emmaus, Pennsylvania

My thanks to:
Sandra for her photographs, Sarah and Viv for their picture research, John for the pattern artwork. In addition, Carol Hemmings for make-up and hair and Sue Duffy for styling on the session, together with models Bisi (from Sarah Cape), Frances Kostan, Leah Seresin, Claire Sharp, Eleanor Thompson, Helen Gibas and Henrietta Winthrop. Also to all my friends who loaned me clothes to draw from and use as research, plus many of the prints and pictures used to illustrate the book; Milly Thompson for photographing Anne Marie Butler's jacket, details of which provide the endpapers; and Sue Bogenor for allowing her curtain to be included as a sampler. Finally, for their unflinching support, Angela Jeffs, my editor, Jill Leman, the designer, both of Overall, and Phoebe Phillips of Phoebe Phillips Editions.

A PHOEBE PHILLIPS EDITIONS BOOK

Edited and designed by Overall Publications
Photographs by Sandra Lousada
Pattern artwork by John Hutchinson
Picture research by Sarah Howell and Viv Adelman
Typeset by TNR Ltd London
Printed in Italy by Arnoldo Mondadori Co Ltd

Library of Congress Cataloging in Publication Data

Thompson, Sue (Susan Jane), 1937-
  Decorative dressmaking.

  "A Phoebe Phillips edition book"--
  Includes index.
  1. Dressmaking.   2. Tailoring (Women's)
  I. Title.
TT515.T49   1985   646.4'04   85-10888
ISBN 0-87857-579-0 hardcover
ISBN 0-87857-580-4 paperback

Contents

Edwardian fashion plate showing various decorative techniques: pintucks, topstitching, flounces, bands and pleats.

8

Introduction

I am often asked how to design clothes; the answer is something of a puzzle. Designing clothes relies on a combination of experience, technical knowledge and imagination. But it is difficult to gain experience without technical knowledge, and vice versa, so I have devised this book to help remedy this situation, by building up the necessary experience through a step-by-step examination of dressmaking techniques, therebye encouraging the last of the three necessary attributes – imagination.

Most dressmaking books lay down rules, offering over-simplified explanations, stifling both independent thought and imagination. My book aims to do exactly the opposite, explaining the principles involved at each stage, so that you will understand not only how to do something, but also why, so enabling you to make your own designs.

The book is divided into ten chapters, each dealing with one decorative technique. The first page of the chapter shows a sampler illustrating what *can* be done by someone with experience. Thereafter the chapter is divided into two parts. The first describes the technique, explaining what it is, how it was used in the past and how to do it, plus ideas and guidlines for designing with it. There are also notes on choosing fabric and how this will affect the technique. Some simple pattern cutting is included; do not take fright! No

previous experience is necessary as there are diagrams explaining exactly how this is done. The second part of the chapter provides an example of a garment incorporating the technique, with all the information needed to make it, and ideas for several variations. There are two ways to make the patterns for these projects. Either follow the instructions (in the second part of the chapter) showing how to adapt a commercial paper pattern. Or turn to the pattern diagrams shown on pages 140–151 – these are scaled down from the actual patterns used to make the clothes – and draw up a pattern for your own size. The advantage of the former method is that a pattern can be chosen which takes account, in its basic shape, of prevailing fashion. For example, at the moment clothes are unstructured and worn very loose, but a tighter, more structured look may well appear in a year or two, and paper patterns do reflect these changes. If on the other hand you want the garment to look exactly like the one in the photograph, then choose the latter method as the diagrams are made from the patterns I used. (The only exception is the fagotted jacket which is made up entirely from rectangular strips of fabric. The diagram for this is given in the chapter itself and not at the back. Numerous drawings are provided in both parts and these should be 'read' alongside the text as they contain more information and tips on making up.

Look through the book at the photographs and illustrations of old and new clothes and then select the technique which interests you most, and read the first part of the chapter, both text and drawings. Next work through the chapter, making up samples of some of the ideas and experiments so that you understand how each works in practice as well as in theory: armed with this experience you will also be able to work out designs of your own.

By this stage you should feel ready either to make up the project, or to make up a garment to your own design. In the second of the cases it is probably a good idea to read through the first part of the other chapters, as there is a certain amount of information which overlaps and may, therefore, be helpful. Before buying any fabric, do please read the whole of the second part of the chapter, together with the notes on fabric in the first part and the 'Notes' at the back of the book.

You will probably have realised by now that this book is for those who enjoy making clothes as much as wearing them, who like experimenting and are not put off by learning new things. It is for the dressmaker who is fascinated by the texture of pintucks, the neatness of bindings, or the fall of flounced fabric, and who enjoys the time spent doing exacting work in order to make a beautiful and unique garment that will last and give pleasure for years.

Flounces

The Oxford Illustrated Dictionary defines a flounce as "an ornamental strip
gathered and sewn by upper edge round woman's skirt etc. with lower edge hanging".
They are wrong. A true flounce is never 'gathered';
the waving free edge is formed by clever cutting of shaped pieces.
However, this is a common misconception. The term "frills and flounces" trips lightly
off the tongue, giving rise to the idea that there is little to choose between the two,
but the difference is akin to that between an overblown cabbage rose and an altar lily.
A frill tends towards silliness whereas a flounce is a more serious and better organised affair
which, at its best, can be quite sculptural in effect.

◀ *The flounces in the sampler on the left are made from thin plastic sheet,
thus avoiding any need to finish the edges. Double-sided sticky tape
was used to joint the flounces and to hold them in place.*

Flounces started early; this girl from Verona was wearing them in the 1st century AD.

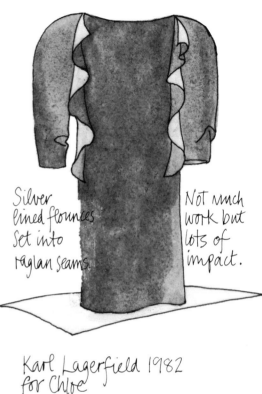

Silver lined flounces set into raglan seams.

Not much work but lots of impact.

Karl Lagerfield 1982 for Chloé

The flounce in fashion

When they re-appeared in the 1920s, after decades of frills, flounces must have appeared highly sophisticated, giving a simpler, smoother outline but still offering a wide variety of decorative finishes. Indeed, the flounce was used so extensively that the name 'flapper' was coined – and a good description it was too, for the woman of style in her new body-freeing tubular dress, which flapped with flounces from every part of her anatomy. Perhaps another reason for

their popularity was that, attached to the front of women's bodices, they conveniently hid the bulging breasts of ladies too well endowed to comply with the current dictates of fashion which demanded a flat silhouette.

The use of flounces died out almost entirely with the onset of the war and although a few did appear in the 1940s, they were generally used only to soften the effect of an otherwise severe outfit. In the 50s and early 60s flounces were practically unknown and it was not until

the advent of 'flower power' and the rise of the hippie movement that a fashion for wearing pre-war clothes revived the softer look of earlier times, and this continues as one of the many strands of fashion up to the present time.

Though the use of flounces is not extensive in the 1980s, who knows what fashion might decree in the coming years. Why not add flouncing to your repertoire of techniques, so that you can leap in when the flounce once more becomes 'de riguer'.

Sprigged muslin, satin, crêpe-de-chine and lightweight woollen suiting used to make a tiered collar, two jabots and a carefully cut flounce set into the yoke of a jacket.

Making flounces

There are nearly as many ways of making flounces as there are types of flounce.

The simplest flounce is just a piece of fabric attached by one side or a point and left to hang freely so that waves form along the free edge.

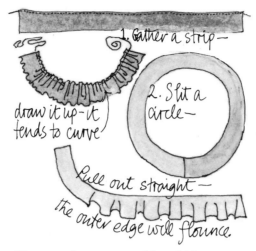

1. Gather a strip —

draw it up — it tends to curve

2. Slit a circle —

Pull out straight — the outer edge will flounce.

Flounces from a curved band The fullness in a flounce is often made by cutting curved bands of fabric so that, when sewn in place, the hanging free edge is longer than the attached edge. This is rather like making a frill without the gathers.

Flounces such as these often form circles and you can vary the amount of flounce by altering the size of the circle used, the increase between the inner and outer circumference being greater on a small circle than a larger one.

● EXPERIMENT – cut a series of flounces of different sizes.
Several small circles can be cut and joined to make very full flounces or collars like the ones Princess Diana made so popular in 1981.

a triangle

an equilateral triangle

a pair of curved flounces

a pair of long triangles

Practise with a silk scarf, or cut some geometric shapes from small scraps of fabrics and use your ingenuity to produce interesting effects.
Neck flounces of this type can also take the form of bows, with even triangular or half-moon shaped pieces of fabric attached in the same way.
Try tacking shaped pieces such as those illustrated on to whatever you happen to be wearing to see how they hang and then adjust them until you produce an effect you really like.

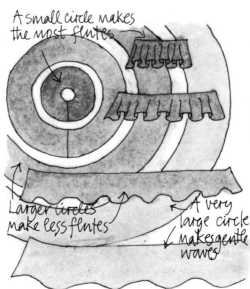

A small circle makes the most flutes

Larger circles make less flutes

A very large circle makes gentle waves

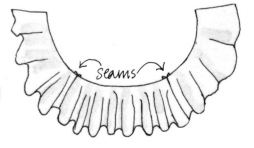

seams

13

1930s
Soft wool suit
with flounced
collar and
sleeves

Controlled flounces Flounces have one great advantage over frills: they are more easily controlled. Every wave can be made to hang exactly where it is required and their size varied to suit the design. To make a collar with a flounce at the centre front to fit a plain round neck, draw up a pattern of the basic collar and then draw in lines exactly where you want folds to fall. Cut through these lines from the outer edge of the pattern to within 1/16in. of the neck line and spread out on another sheet of paper. When made up, this collar will form a flounce as shown in the first illustration.

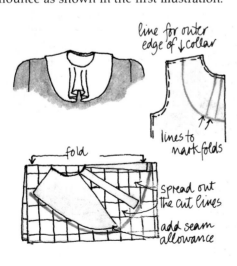

line for outer
edge of ↓collar

lines to
mark folds

fold

spread out
the cut lines

add seam
allowance

● REMEMBER – gravity affects the way flounces hang! They tend to fall vertically however much you have tried to arrange the pattern to create horizontal folds.

● REMEMBER – consider the grain lines carefully. For a flounce to hang the same way either side of the centre line, the grain must run identically on both sides. Therefore the centre line should be cut either on the straight or on the true cross (bias).

More complicated controlled flounces can give a simple looking result. Look at the wool suit illustrated on this page. The flounces are only slightly wavy, and this has influenced the success of the design; if the flounces had been any fuller, the line would have been destroyed.

For the best effect, the waves must fall in the right places. This is no problem on the skirt and sleeves where the seams are straight, but the curve of the neck and the cross-over on the lower right front need special treatment. The best way to do this is to cut patterns for these flounces with every fold worked out in advance.

Lay the front pattern piece on a sheet of paper and draw around the neck edge and down to the hem and across the lower edge of the front as shown. Then mark the stitching line and draw in a line indicating the required width of the flounce. Cut out the piece and cut through from both directions, as illustrated, almost to the stitching line.

Lay the cut up pattern on to another sheet of paper, and spread out the cuts. The amount left between the pieces can be made the same or varied as in this case; it would be a good idea to leave a larger gap where the flounce is pulled across to the other side of the front at the waist.

Draw around the pieces, making a smooth line on the free edge, and adding seam allowances as indicated. Do the same for the back neck flounce, not forgetting to add extra on to the shoulder seams to match the front so that a fold will form nicely on the

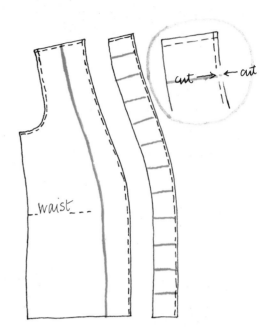

waist

cut → ← cut

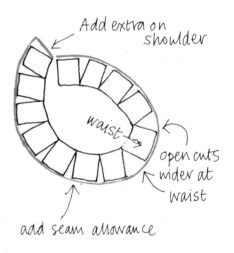

Add extra on
shoulder

waist

open cuts
wider at
waist

add seam allowance

shoulder. Cut out the pattern pieces in spare fabric. As the left front is covered by the right front below the cross-over point, it can be made shorter. Tack the shoulders together on the jacket and flounce, then tack the flounce on to the jacket. Try it on and make any adjustments necessary, altering the pattern to match.

You may find that you have produced a rather weird pattern but do not worry: if it was successful when you tried it out in rough fabric, you know that it is going to work, despite its odd shape.

The lavishly flounced evening coat and dress, far left, was drawn by the German artist Ernst Dryden who worked first in Paris and later moved to the States where he became a successful film dress designer in Hollywood. But I think the animated ladies, photographed at a wedding, are more typical of the way flounces were actually worn in the 1930s. As for Madame Lelong on the left, she is wearing a more fashionable evening version of the day dresses shown above, probably one of her husband's creations.

Some other shapes to try

A spiral makes a good basis for a flounce to be attached to a straight edge or seam, as it is an easy way to graduate the amount of flounce with the most fullness coming at the centre and the least at the outer edge. Although it might take longer to draw the pattern, it saves on fabric and is simple to cut out. The outer edge can be zigzagged before cutting out, thus making it an easy way to finish the free edge.

Two spirals can be joined at the outer ends to make a symmetrical flounce, which could be used for a collar or a skirt hem.

← Join at this end

Flounces can be cut in many other ways, which may look complicated to make up but are not necessarily so. The end result is always well worth the extra effort taken to draw out a difficult shape. The child's dress illustrated has flounces around the hem which are cut as shown and then sewn to the curved lines marked on the skirt. This gives a typically 20s look which could just as easily be used for an adult's dress and would move well when dancing the Charleston!

collar made from two spiral flounces

Cut flounces for this simple shift from the shape below.

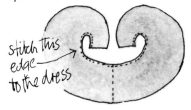

stitch this edge to the dress

Cut two flounces to stitch to the centre front and back, cut two half flounces to stitch to the sides

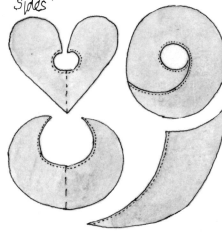

Some more shapes to try

- EXPERIMENT – with different shapes. Be brave. Be bold. See what happens! It may not always turn out as you expected, but if you do not like the first effect, try again. You may accidentally discover an interesting idea or create a wild effect that can be adapted to fit in with your original design.

- REMEMBER – soft fabrics will fall in soft folds and stiff fabrics in stiffer folds, so producing a whole range of effects from one pattern.

How to set on a flounce

There are several different ways in which to do this.

a) The flounce can be sewn flat down on to an edge, e.g. a neckline or hemline which can then be faced in the usual way. The Kenzo dress shown on the opposite page is a good example of this.

b) Where the flounce is going to hang from an edge – perhaps the hem of a skirt or as a cuff – the flounce is laid on the edge, right sides together, and stitched in place. The edges are neatened together and then the seam allowances pressed up under the skirt or cuff. This is how the flounced wool coat below was made.

Wool crêpe coat made for my grandmother in 1939, with slightly flounced collar, sleeves and hem

c) Set the flounce into seams, like those on the front of the dress illustrated on page 12. Stitch to the right side of one side of the seam and then make up the seam in the normal way, but with the seam allowances pressed to one side rather than open.

d) On the child's dress shown on page 16, a placement line is marked on the main garment. The flounce is laid on the dress, right sides together, with the top edge lapping over the placement line by the width of the seam allowance and then stitched in place.

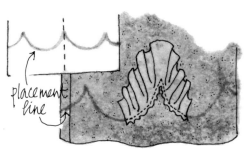

placement line

e) Another easy method to use is to press back the seam allowances on the piece to which the flounce is to be attached, lap this edge over the flounce, pin in place and then stitch.

This technique has the great advantage that when pinned, the garment can be tried on, and the flounce adjusted to hang perfectly before being stitched. The top skirt flounces on the skirt on page 11 have been applied in this way; the lower flounces, however, have been laid on the right side of the dress (i.e. with the wrong side of the flounce on the right side of the dress) and positioned so that the lower edge of the flounce above covers the top edge. They have then been topstitched into position.

f) Sometimes flounces are sewn to the right side of necks or armholes and the edge is then bound.

● NOTICE – that the curved placement line on the child's dress adds to the effectiveness of the flounces by encouraging them to fall in folds. This

mark placement line

pin flounce and stitch

was a common device employed in the construction of the 1920s flapper dress.

● REMEMBER – decide how you are going to attach your flounces as you work out the design of the garment.

● REMEMBER – add a seam allowance to a flounce so that it does not end up narrower than originally intended.

Suitable fabrics

The type of fabric you use for a flounce depends on the design of the garment itself, but obviously those materials which hang well will lend themselves best to the technique. All crêpes – silk, cotton or wool even the thicker woollen types of crêpe – flounce well, as do muslins, chiffons, georgettes and any softly woven cottons and silks. Basically anything that falls in delicious soft folds can be used.

Stiffer fabrics, such as cotton drill, will give a pleasantly waved edge if cut without too much fullness (the Kenzo dress on the right). For theatrical

costumes, however, thick or stiff fabrics can be *very dramatic*, while the large scale of curtains and pelmets will make impressive flounces.

Both plain and patterned fabrics are suitable, but strongly patterned materials should be chosen and cut with care or the design may appear too jumbled. The main fabrics to avoid are those with a noticeably different warp and weft or a strongly twilled (diagonal) weave, as these will all tend to hang unevenly. A good test is to hold up a fabric on the bias and then turn it and hold it up on the opposite bias; if it 'hangs' differently it will probably not make a successful flounce. However, look out for happy accidents – the most unlikely fabrics used in an imaginative way can sometimes give interesting results.

1982 Kenzo

Cotton drill mini dress

wide shoulders and sleeves

Flounced collar and skirt

● REMEMBER – since a flounce shows both sides of the fabric, it should never have too obvious a wrong side. Prints in particular are not always successful though obviously this does not apply to chiffon or other transparent printed fabrics.

● EXPERIMENT – with different fabrics. In the end, it is up to you – your taste and your preference – that dictates the way in which you interpret a design. Why not be the first person to make and wear a flounced mohair coat?

Finishing off the edges

There are a number of ways in which you can finish off the edges of a flounce.

Picot edge In the 1920s the most common finish for a flounce was a picot edging. This is a commercial finish, and in those days the cut pieces of fabric would have been sent off to specialist firms. Today, in the larger towns and cities, it is still occasionally possible to find places that offer such a service.

Zigzag edge This is often just as good, the edge of the fabric either being kept flat or stretched out to create what Zandra Rhodes, the English designer, described as 'lettuce edging', a telling description for a crinkly finish.
Use ordinary sewing thread or a shiny embroidery thread in matching or contrasting colours. Stitch a little way from the edge and then trim, close to the stitches, with very sharp scissors. Sometimes a tiny edge is rolled over before the edge is zigzagged; in this case stitch close to the edge.

● EXPERIMENT – with spare pieces of fabric to determine the right size of stitch to use. Anything from a wide open zigzag to one that is so close it almost resembles satin stitch can prove effective, depending on the material being used and the design of the garment.

Hand rolled edges These make flounced clothes look superb as well as expensive, but are only for the patient and dextrous dressmaker. They have no other advantage over picot or zigzagged edges.

Machined edges Turn back and machine these with straight stitch in the usual way.

Bound edges Use bias strips in matching or contrasting colours and texture (for details, turn to page 39).
Stretch the binding very slightly as you sew it on and, if it is cut on the 'true cross' – that is exactly 45° to the selvedge – it will make a smooth flat

edge which looks equally good from both sides.

Stiffened edges Theatrical costumes or fancy dress clothes sometimes require a dramatic effect which can be achieved by stiffening the edges of flounces. This is done by couching thick threads, such as transparent nylon, or a thin wire – try the type used in millinery – into the hem of the flounce as it is sewn, which will give a strongly undulating effect. You could also use this technique for curtain pelmets.

● EXPERIMENT – with this method. It is the best way to learn what can and cannot be done.

Pinked edges This technique can only be used on fabrics which do not fray, such as felt. You will need a pair of pinking shears! The zigzag edging they make is very distinctive and looks especially good if the flounce is in a different colour to the rest of the outfit.

Lined flounces This is a method that can be used to introduce a contrasting colour or texture to a flounce, as illustrated by the Chloe dress on page 12. Lined flounces are easy to make up and can be 'bagged out'.

BAGGING OUT : *Leave edge to be stitched to the garment open and turn the whole thing right side out through it*

Lay lining on flounce right sides together – and stitch round free edge with the smallest possible seam allowance double stitch and trim corners

● AVOID – using too small a stitch when sewing the two layers together, especially if the fabrics are tightly woven, or you could end up with a rather stiff seam – unless, of course, that is what you want.

● AVOID – using thick fabric for lined flounces, as they will be clumsy.

● REMEMBER – both sides of the flounce will show, so any finish used on the free edge should look good from both sides, though not necessarily the same.

More ideas

Flounces can be used to decorate fancy dress clothes such as pierrots, clowns and Spanish dancers for yourself or your children. Felt will flounce nicely for capes and skirts, while plastic fabrics, cut into fairly subtle flounces, can be used for space-age collars and cuffs.
Use flounces to edge cushions and lightweight curtains instead of the more conventional frills. You could also make flounced pelmets by following the basic principles learned in this chapter.

Finally, the only way to really understand how to cut and use flounces is with practice, cutting up any fabric you can spare – torn sheets, old clothes, even paper.
Make a flounced dress for a baby, a flounced clown suit for a child, a flounced stock for your husband and a flounced jabot for your mother, even a collar for the cat! Then you will begin to know enough to design a flounced dress for yourself.

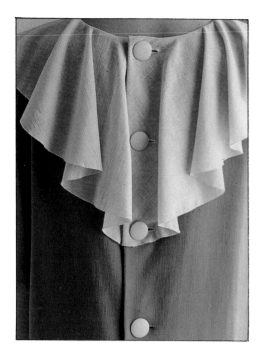

This is an easy adaptation to make and it is also very versatile. I think it works best on a fairly square-shouldered dress, as this provides a foundation from which the flounce can hang, thus encouraging it to form beautiful fluted folds – the very essence of a good flounce. This dress was made from a simple shift pattern, with set-in sleeves fully gathered at the head. However, you could substitute a raglan sleeve with padded shoulders for a similar effect. The sleeves are cut short but could equally well be long, and the whole pattern could be shortened for a shirt or top, or flared from hem to shoulder to make a style suitable for larger sizes or maternity dresses.

Fabric

This dress is made in a Swiss cotton cheesecloth, a lightweight but firm crêpe fabric which hangs well, forming lovely folds on the cross grain. Of course, you could use a heavier or stiffer fabric for the dress and cut the flounce from some lighter material, either matching, contrasting or perhaps of a different pattern or texture. Imagine a sophisticated black wool dress with a flounce cut in black satin.

Note: If you prefer, close the back opening with a zip rather than with buttons.

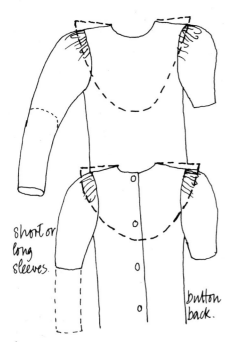

short or long sleeves.

button back.

Fig. 1

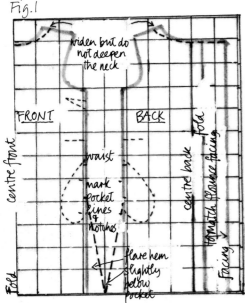

widen but do not deepen the neck

FRONT   BACK

centre front

waist

mark pocket lines & notches

flare hem slightly below pocket

fold

centre back

fold

to match flounce facing

facing

Adapting the basic pattern

Begin by tracing off the pattern pieces that need to be altered on to lightweight pattern paper.
Draw in the alterations as shown in Fig. 1, selecting only those that you need.
Cut out.
Now trace off and cut out the pocket pattern piece.
Lay the front and back on another piece of paper and mark around the neck, shoulder, armhole to waist (Fig. 2). Draw in the line for the outer edge of the flounce and cut out.

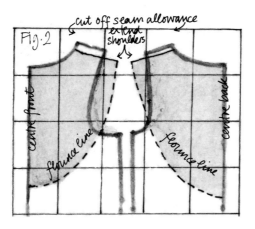

cut off seam allowance

Fig. 2

extend shoulders

centre front

flounce line

centre back

flounce line

Making the flounce pattern

There are two ways in which you can make the flounce pattern.

Method 1 (Fig. 3) is for a pattern with a fairly straight neck and shoulder.

Method 2 (Fig. 4) is for a pattern with a curved neckline.

Whichever method you choose, depending on the style of your basic dress pattern, cut through the lines and lay out the front part of the flounce pattern on a piece of folded paper, with the centre front on the fold, spreading out the cut sections to resemble the rays of the sun (Fig. 5).
Do the same with the back.

For both methods

Work around the pattern piece and draw a new cutting line in an even curve as shown (also Fig. 5).

● DO NOT – draw exactly around the ends of the sections, which are uneven, but draw a new line.

● DO NOT – be put off by the fiddly nature of this exercise – it is easier than it looks.

Add seam allowance and curve the shoulder seam slightly to encourage a fold to form on the shoulder (Fig. 6).
Remember to add the facing to the back.
Note: The grain line is on the bias.

Cutting out

Cut out all the pieces for the garment using the adapted pattern pieces. In

Fig. 3 Method 1 – To use with a straight neck and shoulder

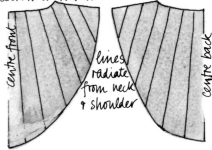

centre front

lines radiate from neck & shoulder

centre back

Fig. 4 Method 2 – to use with a curved neck

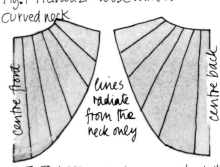

centre front

lines radiate from the neck only

centre back

Fig. 5 For both methods – spread out the rays, use weights to hold the pieces

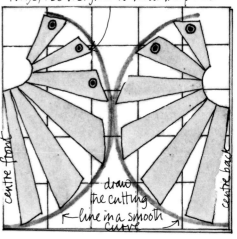

centre front

draw the cutting line in a smooth curve

centre back

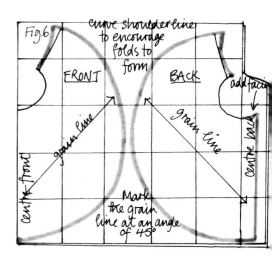

Fig. 6

curve shoulder line to encourage folds to form

FRONT   BACK

add facing

centre front

grain line

grain line

centre back

Mark the grain line at an angle of 45°

main fabric cut out: 1 front, 1 back, 1 pair sleeves, 1 pair of sleeve facings, 2 pairs of pockets. In contrast fabric cut out: 1 front flounce, 1 back flounce, 1 bias strip 1¼in. wide to fit neck.

Making up

Dress Stitch the shoulder and underarm seams.
Stitch the side seams, setting in the pockets.
Gather the sleeve heads and set in the sleeves.

Flounce Join the shoulder seams with a narrow French seam – this will help stiffen the seam so that it stands up slightly, forming a fluted fold over the sleeve head.
Neaten the edge of the flounce. You can do this either by hand, rolling over the edge to the inside and slip stitching or, better still, by zigzagging the edge with a fairly close small zigzag stitch (see page 18 for details of finishes).

● EXPERIMENT – to get the zigzagging right, practising first on small scraps of the same fabric. Do not expect to get it right first time.

● AVOID – stretching the edge.

● AVOID – using too close a stitch as this will stiffen the edge, though this could be an advantage with some fabrics, helping to hold the flounce in nice even flutes at the edge.

EXPERIMENT – try using thicker or thinner thread or shiny embroidery cotton in matching or contrasting colours.
Once you have finished stitching the edge of the flounce, you will need to trim the edge very neatly, take great care not to cut into the zigzag stitching. Sometimes fabric continues to fray for a while, but this should soon stop.

To set on the flounce lay it, right side upwards, on the right side of the dress, matching the centre front, centre back and shoulder notches.
Pin and machine around close to the neck edge using a large stitch (Fig. 7).

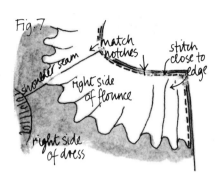

On the back, pin and stitch the edge of the flounce to the edge of the dress, working from the neck edge to the lower edge of the flounce.
Neaten the edge of the back facing from the neck to hem.
On each side of the back, fold the facing on to the wrong side of the dress through the 'foldline' (refer back to Fig. 1) and press firmly.
Now re-fold the facing through this foldline on to right side of the dress at the neck only and pin.
Lay the bias strip on the neck edge, right sides together, starting and finishing 1cm over the facing (Fig. 8).
Pin and stitch around the neck from end to end, i.e. over the facing at the back.
Clip into the seam allowance and turn corners right sides out, so that the facing is folded back on to the wrong side.

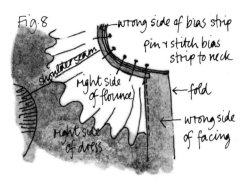

Edge stitch the binding.
Press the seam allowance to the wrong side on the free edge of the binding, stretching the edge as you go.
Press the binding to the wrong side of the dress and pin in place on the dress only (this means lifting the flounce out of the way).
Stitch around close to the edge of the binding, starting and finishing about 1in. into the facing.
Mark and make buttonholes and sew on buttons to correspond. There are six buttonholes in all on the dress shown on page 19, the last one positioned well above the hem.
Turn up the hem.

Note: On some sleeves, you could make a small shoulder pad and stitch it into the dress to project under the sleeve head to add to the wide shouldered effect.

Variations –

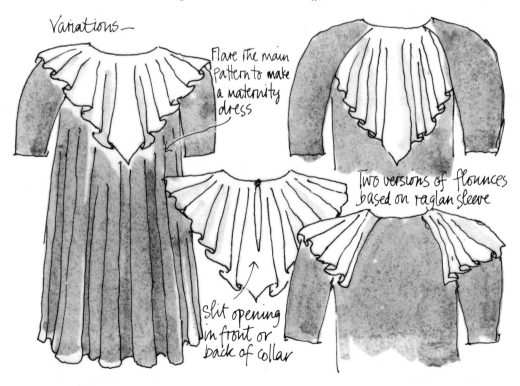

Flare the main pattern to make a maternity dress

Two versions of flounces based on raglan sleeve

Slit opening in front or back of collar

21

Stripes

One of the easiest ways to create an effect in dressmaking is to use striped fabric.
You can do as little or as much as you like, going either for small details or a stronger all-over look.
The simplest dress in a strongly striped fabric will always make an impact.
This chapter outlines the ways in which you can, almost literally, draw with stripes.
Use them to form the structure of a garment or to add simple decoration;
a change of direction is often enough to give interest,
and is well within the range of even the most inexperienced dressmaker.
In contrast, intricate geometric designs can be constructed by someone who not only has experience,
but the patience to fiddle for hours if need be in order to achieve the required effect.
I always find this an enjoyable task, rather in the same way that some people are happy
to spend days putting a large and complex jigsaw together.
Perhaps you may discover some of this same pleasure in working with stripes.

◄ *The advantage of using striped fabrics is that they can be cut, re-arranged and stitched in any number of ways.*
This sampler started out as an exercise in making geometric patterns;
it ended up representing a star, made up of mitred triangles, rising above a range of hills –
single triangles – appliquéd in place with zigzag stitch.

Understanding striped fabric

Before rushing out to buy some material take time to think. Although virtually every stripe is ripe for exploitation, it is worth considering a few basic facts before you go any further, particularly if you are a beginner.

Almost every type of fabric can be striped, so the full range of clothing is open to interpretation in stripes, from ballgowns and dungarees to winter coats and summer dresses.

● REMEMBER – a striped fabric that initially catches your eye might not be suitable for the project you have in mind. It may be too soft or too stiff, too thick or too thin to achieve the effect you are looking for, so always match the weight and feel of the fabric to the decorative technique employed. Read through this chapter before you buy anything.

How fabrics are striped

There are two ways in which fabrics are striped:

a) by being printed onto the surface of a ready-woven fabric

b) by being woven into the fabric itself. Occasionally there are mixtures of the two, so do look carefully!

Printed stripes either run the length of the fabric, parallel to the selvedge (the warp), or across the width to follow the crossways threads (the weft). They are usually straight but can be found doing all manner of strange things: perhaps alternating with floral bands, or zigzagging or waving about, or dashing diagonally across the fabric. Printed stripes are extremely versatile.

● DO – note that every printed stripe has a right and wrong side. The stripes will show up more strongly on the right side (the printed side), than the wrong side where little of the dye may have penetrated the fibres.

● DO– think carefully, therefore, about the way in which you lay out a paper pattern prior to cutting into a printed striped fabric. Since you can only use the right side, it is all too easy to end up with two right sleeves or two left legs

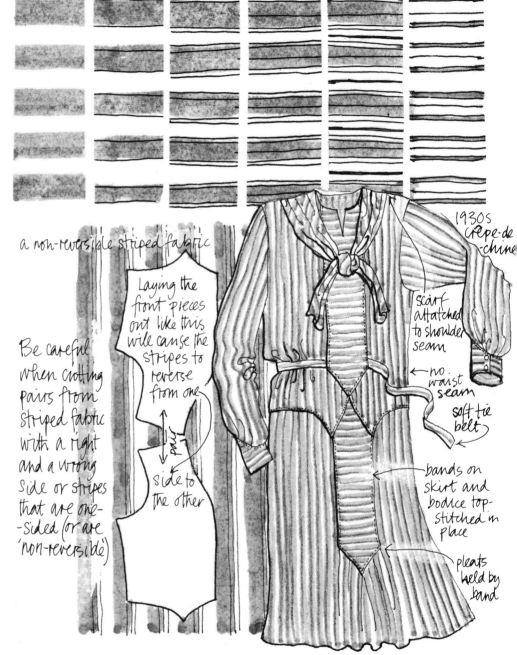

a non-reversible striped fabric

Be careful when cutting pairs from striped fabric with a right and a wrong side or stripes that are one-sided (or are 'non-reversible')

Laying the front pieces out like this will cause the stripes to reverse from one side to the other

pair

1930s crepe-de-chine

scarf attached to shoulder seam

no waist seam

soft tie belt

bands on skirt and bodice top-stitched in place

pleats held by band

instead of the required pair. Plan accordingly.

Woven stripes generally run down the length of the fabric parallel to the selvedge, but occasionally across it. They are almost invariably straight but can be as varied in their colouring as the printed stripe, sometimes more so! Woven stripes can be self-coloured, the texture of the weave forming the stripe – self-coloured satin stripes alternating with twill stripes, for example. Colour,

and therefore striped detail, can be introduced either in the warp, giving lengthways stripes, or in the weft, giving stripes across the fabric.

● DO – be aware that unlike printed striped fabric, woven stripes *can* look the same on both sides. In other words, there is not necessarily a right or wrong side. This means you can use both sides as the right side when cutting out, which makes it easier to match the stripes and, incidentally, saves fabric.

1930s striped 'art silk' or viscose with interesting use of stripes - easy to transpose to a modern garment

separate peplum cut on the bias

weird little pleats →

Left: A wonderful striped sunsuit with wide trousers from the 1930s. Notice how badly the stripes have been matched on the back of the halter neck; the self fabric covered buttons simply add to the confusion! Despite all this the stripes still look interesting. Top: The actress Gertrude Lawrence wearing a striped wool dress and jacket, also 1930s.

Designing with stripes

Before deciding on your design, hold up the fabric you have chosen in front of you and look in the mirror. Play around with your material, arranging the stripes so that they run vertically, horizontally or diagonally. This will give you a clear idea as to what the pattern can and cannot do. For example, a particular

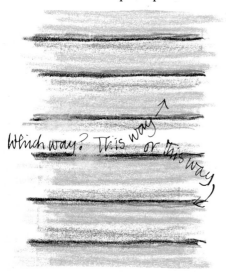

Which way? This way or this way

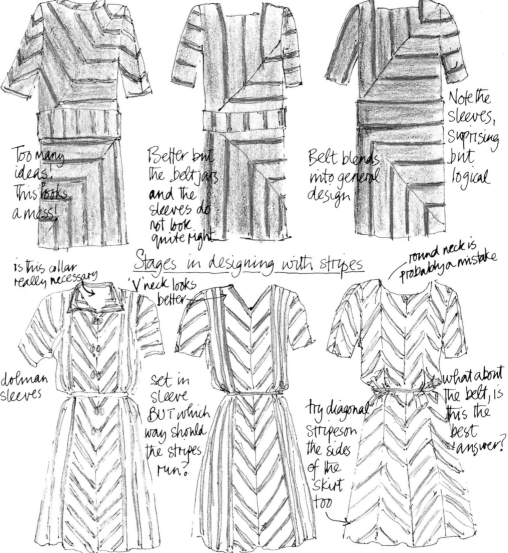

Too many ideas. This looks a mess!

Better but the belt jars and the sleeves do not look quite right.

Belt blends into general design

Note the sleeves, surprising but logical

Stages in designing with stripes

is this collar really necessary

'V' neck looks better

round neck is probably a mistake

dolman sleeves

set in sleeve BUT which way should the stripes run?

try diagonal stripes on the sides of the skirt too

what about the belt, is this the best answer?

stripe used horizontally may sometimes exaggerate the width of the garment, or look better one way up rather than the other.

Expect to take time and trouble when working out a design. Look at the striped clothes illustrated throughout this chapter, and any other drawings or

photographs you come across, even the clothes people are wearing in the streets or displayed in shop windows. Make notes and sketches; file away ideas or references that could be a source of inspiration for future projects.

● DO – relate the way you use stripes in one part of a garment with the way you use them in another. For instance, if using diagonal stripes on a sleeve, try to balance this with a similar use on the skirt and bodice. Trimming a skirt in one way, the bodice using a second technique and the sleeve yet another will only result in a bad design.

● DO – sketch your original idea in several different ways. Then decide on the one you think works best.

Above: A French beach dress by the French
designer Rodier, dated 1922. The striped material
has been cut on the cross and joined to form a
chevron pattern.

Left: Designs from the 1930s by Ernst Dryden.
The figure on the right shows a fine use of striped
fabrics.

Colour in stripes

Woven and printed stripes come in many different combinations of colour; the simplest consists of a single colour on a plain background, alternating across the fabric. By varying the width, and adding other colours, more complex stripes can be devised. Perhaps the most complicated would be a multi-coloured striped fabric, with the stripes varying across the full width of the fabric without a repeat.

Two further categories that printed and woven stripes fall into are:
a) reversible stripes
and
b) non-reversible stripes.
To see what this means, start by making a copy of the stripes shown. Cut the stripes in half and turn one piece round so that the stripes match once more, these are reversible stripes. Now do the same with the second set of stripes illustrated and you will see that the stripes cannot be matched. These then are non-reversible stripes. To avoid ending up with a muddled jumble, try some experiments. Draw more stripes – both reversible and non-reversible – on pieces of paper large enough to cut miniature pattern pieces from (e.g. right and left front, sleeves, skirt pieces etc.). Experiment with them until you have worked out how to make the seams match. Trial and error and common sense, together with illustrations given will help. It is fairly easy to match up reversible stripes so start with these. Then try with non-reversibles.

● REMEMBER – The easiest striped fabric to use and match is one with no right or wrong side; this means you can use either side as the 'right' side when you cut out. Draw more stripes on transparent paper. Cut two left sleeves from it, with the stripe in exactly the same place on both. Turn one over to make a right sleeve and, hey presto, you have a pair! The striped dress project later in the chapter was cut from fabric of this type using this technique, which certainly made it much easier to match the pieces.

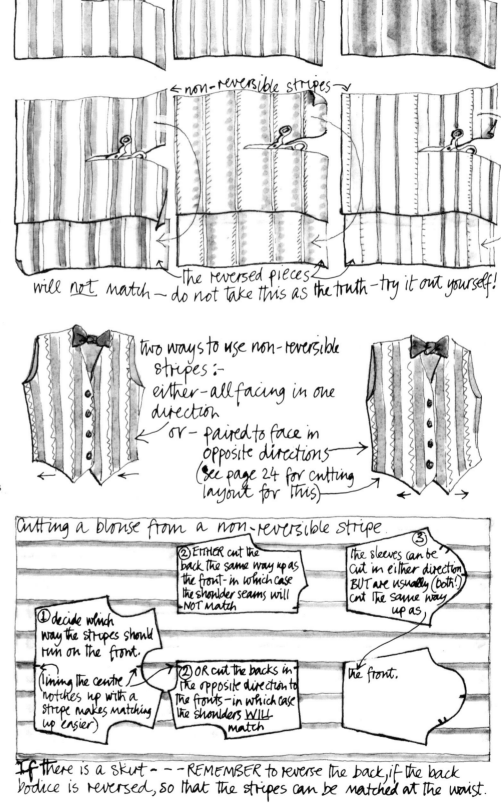

← reversible stripes →

← non-reversible stripes →

will **not** match – the reversed pieces do not take this as the truth – try it out yourself!

two ways to use non-reversible stripes:-
either – all facing in one direction
or – paired to face in opposite directions
(see page 24 for cutting layout for this)

Cutting a blouse from a non-reversible stripe

① decide which way the stripes should run on the front.
(lining the centre notches up with a stripe makes matching up easier)

② EITHER cut the back the same way up as the front – in which case the shoulder seams will NOT match

② OR cut the backs in the opposite direction to the fronts – in which case the shoulders WILL match

③ the sleeves can be cut in either direction BUT are usually (both!) cut the same way up as,

the front.

If there is a skirt – – –REMEMBER to reverse the back, if the back bodice is reversed, so that the stripes can be matched at the waist.

- A USEFUL TRICK – if cutting a simple garment and using a non-reversible stripe: cut the fabric in half lengthways, reversing one half, and then seaming the pieces together again before laying out the pattern pieces.

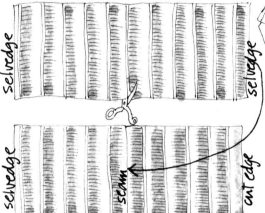

Buying striped fabric

When you go shopping, try to have some idea of which categories of stripes are the most economical and which are less so. Do not, however, expect to be able to work out exactly how much fabric you need for a particular design in advance. Indeed you may not want to work out your design until you have chosen a fabric. Spare pieces can be used up afterwards in many ways. Striped cotton fabrics are often very cheap and can be just as effective as expensive ones.

Here are some other points to remember:

- a narrow reversible stripe will take less fabric than a wider reversible stripe
- a non-reversible stripe will always take more fabric than a reversible stripe, and the wider or more irregular the stripe, the more fabric you will need
- a striped fabric which is the same on both sides (i.e. has two 'right sides'), will use less fabric than the same type of striped material with a right and wrong side
- a paper pattern will seldom allow any extra fabric for matching stripes, so you will need to allow for this.

Look at the wide variety of striped fabrics in the shops and you will quickly learn to tell the difference between the reversibles and non-reversibles, the prints from the weaves, and to appreciate the potential of each.

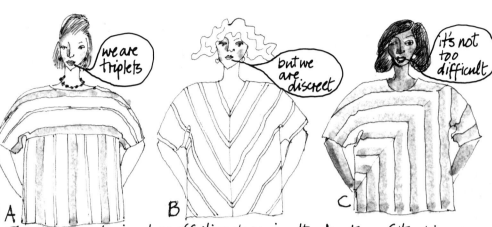

Three blouses showing how effective changing the direction of the stripe can be. They can all be made from the same direction - see below.

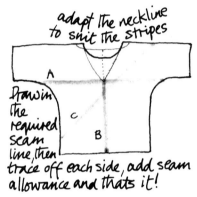

adapt the neckline to suit the stripes

Draw in the required seam line, then trace off each side, add seam allowance and that's it!

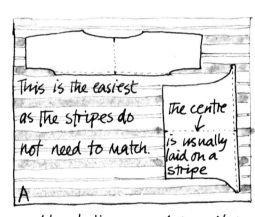

This is the easiest as the stripes do not need to match.

the centre is usually laid on a stripe

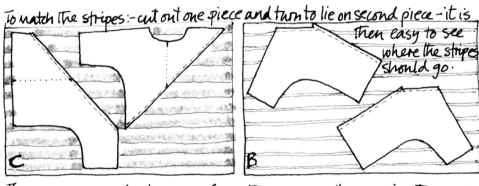

To match the stripes:- cut out one piece and turn to lie on second piece - it is then easy to see where the stripes should go.

Three more examples to make from the same pattern, using the same method.

Designing with stripes

There are any number of ways in which you can use stripes for a dramatic effect. The drawings show three of the many possibilities that are easy to adapt from paper patterns.

Mark a seamline on the pattern, cut through and add a seam allowance on each edge. Work out carefully how to cut the striped fabric you have selected and finally go ahead and make it up.

● DO – use a double pattern for this (that is one that has both sides or halves of the front and back etc.). This makes it much easier to see what you are doing.

● AVOID – trying to be too clever. If a striped pattern is designed to fill the width of the fabric and is noticeably one-sided, as in the overblouse shown above, then use the full width of the fabric for a simple design; the cutting layout is also shown.

● REMEMBER – always give yourself enough time at the beginning of a project to work out the design, find and adjust the pattern, and lay it out on the fabric. Decorative dressmaking should never be rushed; expect to take a reasonably long time right from the start and you will not be disappointed by the results.

Mitred stripes This is an excellent way to 'draw' with stripes. Look at the first two sketches on the previous page. The V-shaped stripes are mitred, that is two pieces of fabric have been assembled to form an angled joint. This can be done on a much smaller scale with narrower stripes to give the sort of effect seen in the project on page 32. To gain maximum effect, the stripe must match precisely at the seams. To do this successfully, they must be at the same angle on each side of the seam.

To make a mitred triangle, take a triangle as illustrated, bring two sides together and make a crease. Open it out. Cut through the crease and add seam allowances on each side as shown. Using the pieces as a pattern, and making sure the sides marked A and B are lying exactly on the same stripe, cut out; then place the two pieces together and stitch the mitred seam.

These mitred triangles can be used in lots of ways. One side of a triangle can be set into a seam and the other two sides appliquéd in place. Or try some of the shapes illustrated and consider ways in which they can be used: as pockets, as borders, adapted for collars, to decorate furnishings, and so on.

Three uses for mitred triangles

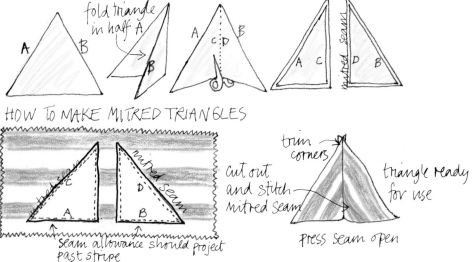

HOW TO MAKE MITRED TRIANGLES

fold triangle in half

trim corners

cut out and stitch mitred seam

triangle ready for use

press seam open

seam allowance should project past stripe

SOME MORE MITRED SHAPES
use the same principle as used for the triangle

Turning stripes Another form of mitring. This method works best with fairly narrow simple stripes, and was much used on the cheap rayon dresses of the 1930s and 40s. Sometimes the manufacturers did not bother to match the stripes, but they were still effective, with endless variations on the same theme.

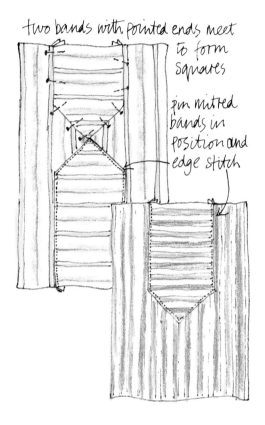

two bands with pointed ends meet to form squares

pin mitred bands in position and edge stitch

To make a turned stripe, cut the pattern for say a band to the required shape and size and mitre the end accurately. Add seam allowances. Cut out carefully, press all the seam allowances to the wrong side and lay in position on the garment. Topstitch all round, close to the edges, with matching thread.

If a band is flared at the hem, spread the gores before stitching so that the band only overlaps the seam allowance on the gore.

● DO – try to appliqué bands, such as these, in place as it makes it much easier to see what you are doing. If you try setting them into ordinary seams working from the wrong side, you will find it almost impossible to match up the stripes.

Pleated stripes These are particularly effective on skirts where part of the pleat is stitched down, with the stripes arranged so that the darker stripe is on top and the lighter one hidden away inside the pleat. This can also be used on sleeves and bodices.

Plain fabric for stripes

If you are lucky enough to find the same fabric in two or more complementary colours, why not make your own striped fabric? This could be time consuming unless you go for a bold approach using fairly wide strips of fabric.

Draw lines on your pattern to indicate where you want the stripes, cut and add seam allowances on each side and cut from the different fabrics. Of course you can add some subtle shaping to these seams without spoiling the striped effect.

Stripes for bindings and pipings

Stripes can be cut on the bias to make bindings and piped edgings for furnishings and clothes, giving a bright barber's pole effect. These show up best juxtaposed with plain fabrics, but give interesting results with prints too.

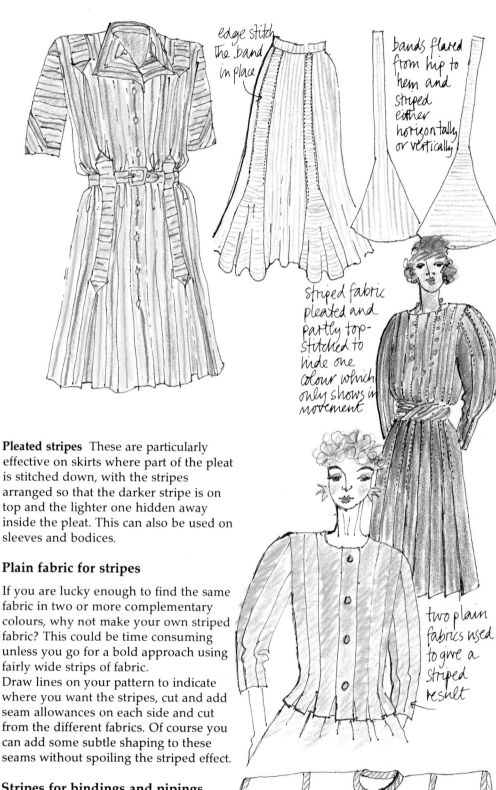

edge stitch the band in place

bands flared from hip to hem and striped either horizontally or vertically

striped fabric pleated and partly top-stitched to hide one colour which only shows in movement

two plain fabrics used to give a striped result

a little striped binding goes a long way!

The main features of this dress, which is similar front and back, are a wide chevron band at hip level and mitred triangles appliquéd to the shoulders and around the neckline, with the fabric tucked and topstitched to hide the pink and show the blue stripes. Two inverted pleats are added to the bodice, with the pleat backs cut so that the stripes run horizontally. The six pleats on the skirt are made in the same way (Fig. 2).

Size

This style will suit those of you with not too much bust. The more bust you have, the more pleats will open at the front; to overcome this problem the dress could be made without pleats.

The hipband has been worked out to fit hips measuring 35–37in, with a finished measurement of 38in. For larger and smaller sizes you will have to make adjustments. Whether the dress will suit you is very much a matter of proportion: you will look fine whether you are 5ft. 4in. tall with 34in. hips, 5ft. 8in. with 36in. hips, or 6ft. with size 44in. hips.

Note: The hip band should not fit too tightly; this would stop the dress hanging properly.

Notes on making the dress

Though not for the complete beginner, this dress is within the range of any dressmaker who is used to working successfully with paper patterns.

● DO – read *all* the instructions before you buy the fabric or start to adapt the pattern.

● DO – make the dress in the order given. This has been carefully worked out so that you are working on the smallest pieces possible, to avoid dragging the whole garment through the machine when, for instance, applying the appliquéd triangles and chevron hip band.

● DO – expect to work *very* accurately. If you are even a few sixteenths out on the chevron band pattern, this will be multiplied by six (there are six parts to the band) and it will end up not fitting onto the main part of the dress.

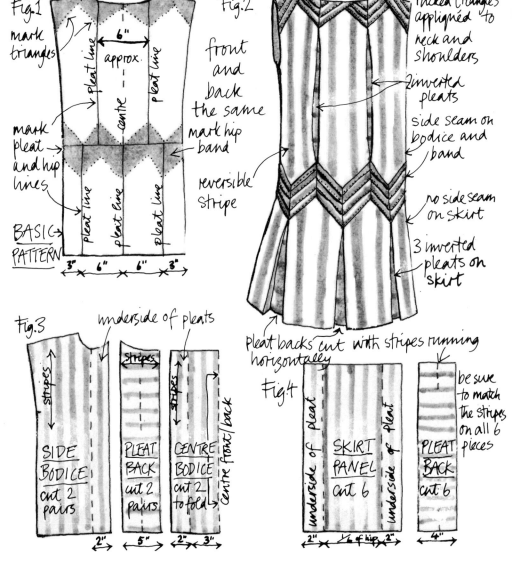

● DON'T – try to make this dress in a rush. It will take lots of time!

Fabric

You can use virtually any firmly woven lightweight fabric which has a similar warp and weft (i.e. it does not have thick threads running across the fabric and thin running down, or vice versa). The fabric used for the dress shown in the photograph is a crisp silk with groups of pink and blue stripes; though many other striped fabrics would be equally successful. As far as the amount of fabric required is concerned, it is impossible to go by the amount given in the basic pattern. Material measuring 4yds. by 40in. wide was used in this instance, but you may need more or less,

depending on the stripes you choose, whether you are going to tuck the hip band and triangles, or whether pleats are to be included in the bodice or not.

The pattern

Choose a straight shift dress pattern with the front and back similar. Or use the diagram given on page 141 to draw up a pattern.

Adapting the pattern

Bodice If your pattern is different front and back, you will need to make separate patterns, but the method remains the same. Cut through the pattern at hip level (Fig. 1). Decide whether you are going to incorporate pleats in the bodice and, if so, mark

vertical lines on your original pattern to show where you intend them to be. They should be the same width apart as the two middle top points on the hip band. Next, either cut through the paper pattern, or trace off each side of the marked line. Add 2in. (Fig. 3) for the underside of the pleat, then make the pattern for the pleat back.

Skirt Use the skirt part of the original pattern as a guide to the finished hip size, which in this instance will fit the hip band pattern made up to 38in. (finished size).
The skirt is made up of six panels of equal size, with inverted pleats between them (Fig. 2).
Note: the pleats on the skirt do not match those on the bodice – this is because the hip band has two points on the top and three below.

Divide the finished measurement by six, i.e. 38in. ÷ 6 = 6⅜in.
Study Fig. 4 and draw up the skirt. Mark the grainlines (stripes) on the skirt panels so that they run vertically, and on the pleat backs so that they run horizontally (Fig. 4).

Mitred triangles These can be applied whether the bodice is pleated or not. On the original pattern bodice, mark the pleat line (Fig. 1) even if you are not going to use it.
Mark in the triangles as shown in Fig.5. Trace off triangle A and cut out. Trace off triangle C, mark it as such and then cut out (Fig. 6). Fold triangle A so that the outer edges come together and draw

a line along the crease (Fig. 7). This will be the mitred seamline. Mark A and B as shown; cut through the seamline (Fig. 7). Draw round pieces A, B and C and add ⅜ in. seam allowances as shown in Fig. 8. Mark the grainlines (i.e. the stripe), and mark A, B and C.

Hip band The band is made in two identical pieces, one front and one back. The example given is for a finished measurement of 38in. to fit sizes 35in.– 37in. Divide the finished measurement into four, i.e. 38in. ÷ 4 = 9½in. Decide on the finished total depth of the band, say 7in.
Fold a piece of printed pattern paper, marked in inch squares, so that you can draw up the rectangle shown in Fig. 10.

● NOTE – The fold in the paper will represent the centre front/centre back, so only a quarter of the band is given.

Mark the rectangle as shown, drawing in the dotted lines. Then, using the squares printed on the pattern paper to guide you, draw in the lines at an angle of 45° as indicated in Fig. 10. Pin both layers together and cut out very carefully. Unpin and check that both halves match exactly. Cut along the dotted lines almost to the edge (Fig. 11); each piece will be 2¾ in. wide. Draw two lines parallel and 2¾ in. apart on the pattern paper (Fig. 12). Lay the cut pieces from Fig. 11 onto it, pulling them out to lie on a straight line.
Draw around them using a ruler, then add seam allowances of ⅜ in.
Cut out, cutting V-shaped notches where indicated (Fig. 12).

● NOTE – you can make the band to a different width to suit the stripes on your fabric.

Cutting out

Before cutting out the hip band make tucks to give a one-colour effect (see the instructions on page 105). Fold tucks in place and press. Topstitch close to the edge of each tuck.
Cut two pieces for the hip band (Fig. 12). Remember to cut the notches, and to check the cut pieces against the pattern for accuracy and to trim if necessary.

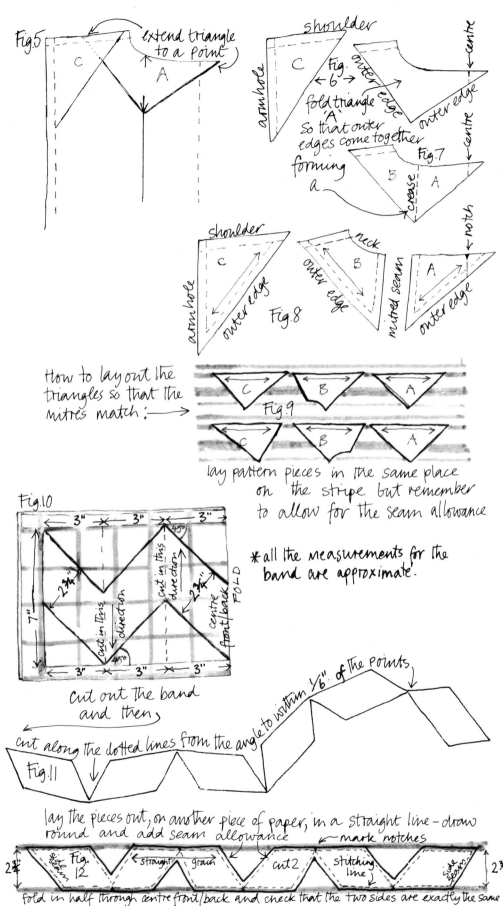

● IMPORTANT – these pieces must be 100 per cent accurate.

Cut the bodice so that the stripes run vertically on the main pieces and horizontally on the pleat backs. Cut out the skirt so that the stripes are vertical on the six panels and horizontal on the pleat backs, remembering also to match up the stripes on the pleat backs.
Cut out the mitred triangles A, B and C. Use tucked fabric if required. These must also be extremely accurate, so check them against the pattern after cutting; trim if required. Cut two pairs of each piece using Fig. 9 as a guide and making sure to lay the grainlines on the same stripe for each piece so that they match.

Making up the dress

Band Fold back one end as shown in Fig. 13. Then stitch from the fold to the seam allowance (but not to the edge of the fabric) backstitching firmly at each end (Fig. 14).
Fold the next section in the same way, stitch. Repeat until all five mitred seams have been completed on both pieces. Press all the seams open, then press the seam allowance on the outer edges to the wrong side. These two pieces can now be joined at the side seams. Note it may be necessary to shape the seams slightly at the top (Fig. 15).

Pleats in front and back of bodice Press the underside of all four pleats, through the foldlines, to the wrong side (Fig. 16). Lay the bodice, with wrong sides uppermost, the pressed foldlines coming together, and the undersides of the pleats on top (Fig. 16). Place the pleat backs in place with their wrong sides uppermost and pin in position. Turn to the right side and check that the pressed edges come together. Stitch, then neaten the edges together.

Mitred triangles Join pieces A and B at the mitred seam edges. With right sides together, stitch from the top to the stitching line at lower edge (not to edge of fabric), as illustrated in Fig. 17. Press the seams open, press the seam allowances on the lower edges to the wrong side, then trim the seam

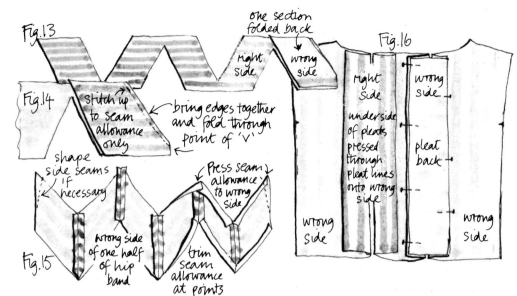

allowance at the points. Lay on the neck edge, using the pattern as a guide, and overlapping as shown in Fig. 18. Topstitch each piece close to the edge in the order shown. Tack the other edges down close to the edge at the neck and shoulders.

Bodice Make up the shoulders and side seams in the usual way. Face the neckline and armholes as instructed in the original pattern.

Skirt Make up the skirt as shown (Fig. 19). Press the underside of the pleats to the wrong side on each skirt panel through the foldlines.
Lay the panels as indicated, then lay the pleat backs in place and pin in a similar way to those made on the bodice. Stitch all six pleats.

Set on the band Lap the top of the band over the bodice and, keeping it level, pin in place, matching points to pleats and side seams. Lap the lower edge of the band over the skirt and again keeping it level, pin in place matching points to pleats. Try on the dress and adjust so that the band lies flat. Topstitch all round very close to the edge.

Hem and finishing off To make the hem you will need to unpick a little way up each pleat seam. Press each piece up by the required amount, re-sew the pleat seams and sew up the hem. Cut away any surplus on the wrong side of the band and oversew or zigzag all the edges.

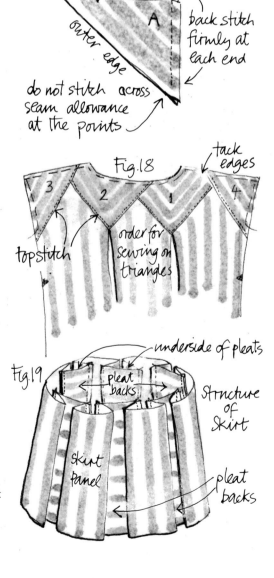

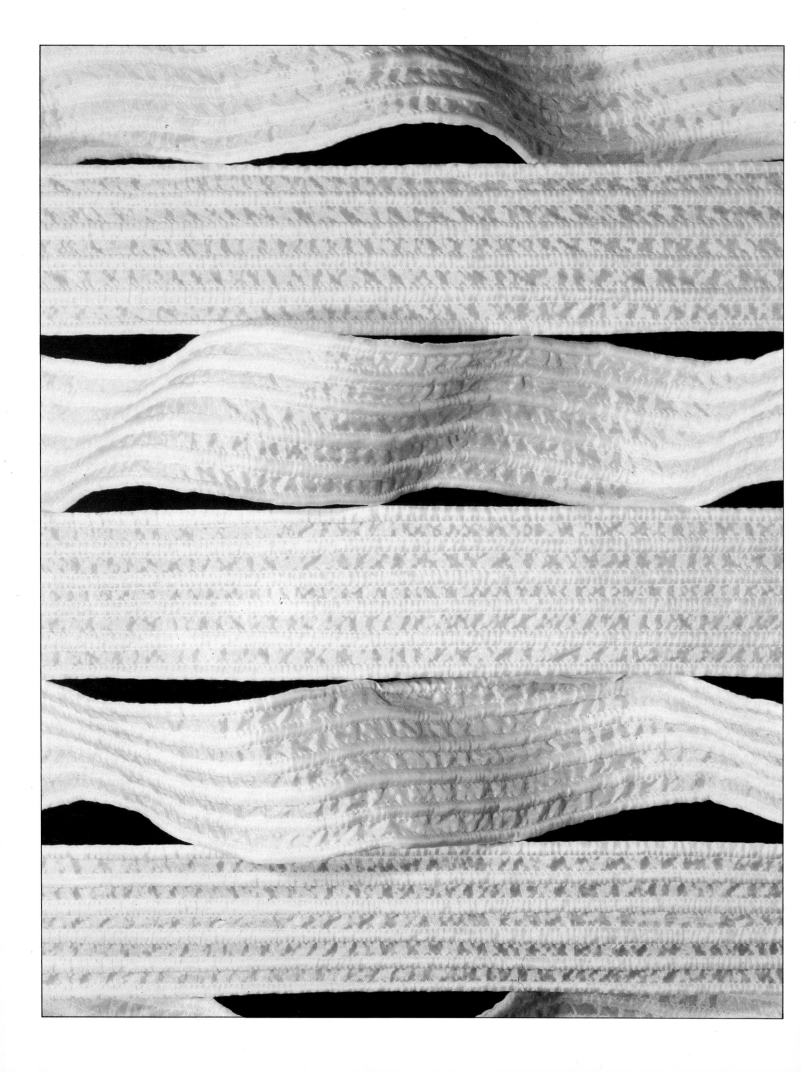

Piping

Piping has been around for a long time, and its continuing use reflects its effectiveness.
At the age of three, I had a cream coloured shantung frock
with red piping and buttons.
By the time I was ten I had a black piped saddle for my horse
and my mother had a 'New Look' dress of black moiré,
piped with shocking pink.
And now my ancient sofa has a striped loose cover with barber's pole piping
and is heaped with fatly piped cushions.

◀ A small detail from a screen by Phyllis Ross. Strips of silk have been piped using the Italian quilting method
and then these have been attached to each other at certain points, leaving the remaining parts free.
The finished effect is strongly three-dimensional , which contrasts with the fine delicacy of the fabric and stitching.

This technique began as a method of reinforcing articles which would be hard worn. Gradually however its intrinsic decorative quality was recognised and this soon gave rise to its use entirely as decoration, illustrated by the child's frock and moiré dress mentioned on the previous page. The rather dreary colour of the former was completely eclipsed by its colourful piping, whilst the black of the latter had a flamboyant air introduced by the decorative effect of the shocking pink piping. Such things as saddles, suitcases and satchels are piped for functional reasons – the piping reinforces the edges – whereas sofas and cushions are piped for a combination of the functional and decorative attributes.

Comparatively inexperienced dressmakers will find that piping is a fairly easy way to give a fillip to their work. If you make a garment from a pattern you have used before but pipe the seams, the effect will be quite different. Of course it is more work, but not difficult, especially if you follow the clues and tips given in the following pages.

Fabric tube enclosing a cord this makes a nice fat round piping

Fabric tube without the cord makes a flat piping

Ready-made piping

can be plain or patterned

Matching striped fabric

Striped fabric trimming plain

Striped fabric trimming floral fabric

Stripes trimming spots

What is piping?

Piping is a cord enclosed in a narrow strip of fabric, or it can be just a tube of fabric. You can buy ready-made piping from any haberdashery department with a fat pipe attached to a plain tape.

Piping cord

This is widely available from haberdashery departments in graded gauges ranging from the very thick to the very thin. It is usually made from a soft white cotton and the thicker the gauge, the less tightly it is twisted so that it does not become stiff. If commercial cord is unavailable, or is too soft or too stiff, knitting wool, embroidery threads or string of a suitable thickness can be substituted.

Fabrics to use for piping

You will have realised by now that as most types of garments can be piped, then it must be true that most types of fabric can be used too. But beware! If you use thick or stiff fabrics you may end up making something a sailmaker or saddler would be proud of, but which might not be a comfortable prospect as clothes. Thick cotton canvas wrapped around a thick cord is probably going to look more like something a plumber would make rather than a dressmaker!

Dress weight cottons are usually ideal and are most effective if of a different colour or fabric from that used for the main part of the garment. Aim for contrasts of texture and pattern as well as colour. Use satin or silk on wool, ciré cotton on plain cotton, diagonal stripes on vertical stripes, stripes on checks and so on. There are as many ideas as there are fabrics, so look around; you should be able to find inspiration for piping some of the fabrics you have already.

Striped fabrics can be used in lots of different ways. There are also many interesting effects to explore using patterned fabric, particularly for children's clothes. The main point to remember is that nothing looks worse than piping that is too thick or too stiff for a garment, either because the wrong fabric or cord has been used. The balance between the two must be right.

Patterned piping trimming plain fabric

Matching fabric used for the piping

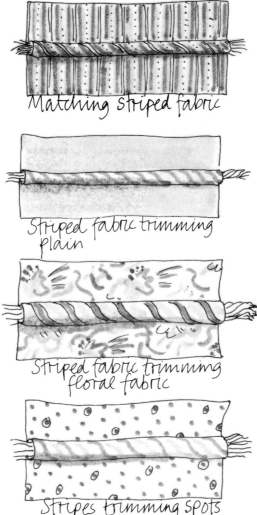

1982

Azzedine Alaia.
Close fitting black wool dress shaped with diagonal piped seams

'wring' or wriggle after stitching. To find this angle, fold the fabric in half lengthways, bring the selvedges together and smooth out the fabric so that it lies flat and the folded edge does not twist. Make a notch close to the higher corner in both selvedges, then open out the fabric and smooth it so that it lies flat. Draw a straight line between the two notches. Now fold the selvedge across onto this line, make a crease and cut through. This is the 'bias' or 'cross' grain.

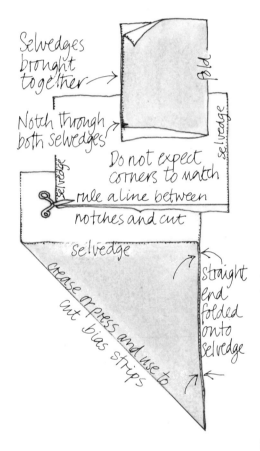

Selvedges brought together

Notch through both selvedges

Do not expect corners to match

rule a line between notches and cut

selvedge

selvedge

selvedge

fold

straight end folded onto selvedge

crease or press and use to cut bias strips

Strips are cut parallel to this line for piping. The width of the strips should be enough to wrap around the cord, plus twice the width of the seam allowance which should be the same as that allowed on the relevant seam.

To make the piping

Fold the binding strip around the cord with the right side of the fabric showing. Then pin and tack in position

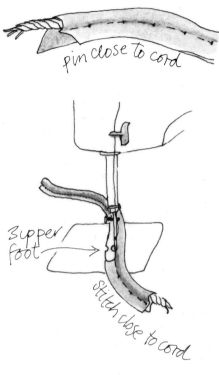

pin close to cord

zipper foot

stitch close to cord

stretching it slightly. Using the piping foot (one-sided or zipper foot), stitch tight up against the cord. It is usually possible to dispense with pinning and tacking after some practice – just fold a short length of the bias strip around the cord, stitch, fold the next part of the strip around the cord and stitch again, repeating until the end.

● AVOID – pulling the top edge of the bias binding over the lower edge. This causes the binding to twist or wriggle and it must be kept smooth and flat.

● AVOID – using any fabric where the warp and weft threads are very different. Such materials have an inexplicable tendency to twist when used for piping, even if cut exactly on the bias.

● NOTE – that if, despite all your precautions, the binding still tends to twist, it may be that this particular fabric is not suitable for cutting on the bias (some fabrics just seem to have a will of their own!) or it may be that the fabric is too thick or thin in relation to the cord.

● EXPERIMENT – with this balance between fabric and cord. For instance, lawn used with a thick cord will look too insubstantial; used with a fine cord it should be fine.

● WASHING – check whether the cord is washable when you buy it – it usually is – and whether it is pre-shrunk. Wash it if not, unless the finished garment is to be dry-cleaned. The fabrics used in conjunction with such a cord should also be pre-shrunk, so if there is any doubt, wash the fabric too before starting to cut it out.

Cutting the outer covering

The outer covering of the piping cord is always cut on the bias or cross of the fabric, that is at an angle of 45° to the selvedge. It is important to do this accurately as otherwise the fabric will

Above: A Victorian fashion plate, dated 1868, showing a daydress with piped seams.

Left: A successful modern use of piping, by the French designer Lanvin.

1930s printed muslin

red piping giving a sailor's collar effect

Band sits just below the waist

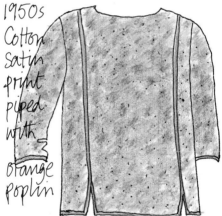

1950s Cotton Satin print piped with orange poplin

1950s

Cotton hopsack; piped collar, bow and seams

Thread

Apart from avoiding very thick thread, which might make the seams bulky, any ordinary thread can be used.

Stitches

There are three lines of stitching on each piped seam: the first row holds the bias strip round the cord; the second holds the piping to one side of the seam; the third makes the actual seam. The first two should be stitched with a large machine stitch (or tacked) and the third with the largest stitch consistent with holding the seam firmly.

● NOTE – small stitches tend to stiffen seams.

Setting piping into a seam

Lay the made-up piping on the right side of the fabric on one side of the seam and pin in place.
Stitch with a large stitch, close to the edge using the piping foot.
Lay the second side of the seam over the piping, right sides together, and pin.
Again using the piping foot, stitch close to the cord, thus making the seam.

● AVOID – stretching the fabric on to the piping.

Ironing

Open out and press all the seam allowances to one side – the piping will automatically turn in the opposite direction. Use the point of the iron, pushing it up against the piping.

● AVOID – ironing over the piping as this will flatten it, and the whole point is that it should stand out roundly.

Piping round curves and corners

Pin the piping onto the side of the seam on which it will finally lie and then stitch close to the piping. Be particularly careful with corners.

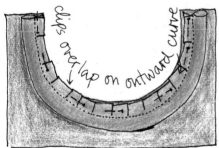

clips spread apart on inward curve

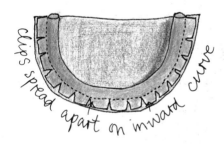

clips overlap on outward curve

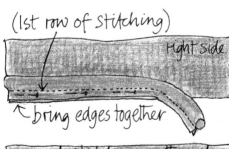

(1st row of stitching)

right side

← bring edges together

and stitch near the edge (2nd row of stitching)

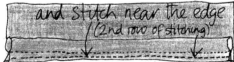

piping between two sides of seam

right side

wrong side

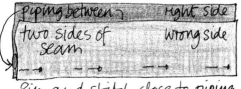

Pin and stitch close to piping (3d row of stitching)

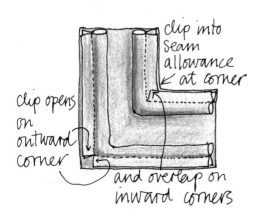

clip into seam allowance at corner

clip opens on outward corner

and overlap on inward corners

Setting piping into edges

This is done in the same way as for setting piping into seams, until the pressing stage. Do this in the normal way for edges, either turning right side out for collars, bands and cuffs etc., or by folding the facing back onto the wrong side of the garment and pressing firmly, again remembering to avoid pressing over the piping. The facings, undercollar etc., can be edgestitched in the usual way.

Cutting down on bulk

As piping involves two extra layers of fabric, there may be a problem, especially if thicker fabrics are being used. The best way to deal with this is to start with a fairly wide seam allowance and after the seam is stitched, to trim the different layers back, grading them from wide to narrow as shown, thus reducing the amount of fabric in the seam.

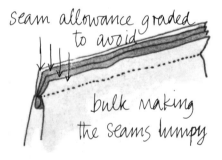

Seam allowance graded to avoid bulk making the seams lumpy

Using ready-made piping

Besides making your own piping, it is usually possible to find a selection of ready-made pipings in large haberdashery shops or department stores. These can be used in the same way as those you make yourself. Occasionally a market stall may be found that specialises in trimmings of all sorts, amongst which there may be a few pipings for dressmaking. Always check whether they are washable or must be dry-cleaned. These manufactured pipings and braids are often made in beautiful colours and from lovely glossy threads.
Occasionally they may be striped – barber's pole fashion. If you see anything special, buy now to use later!

Checked cotton suit with ric-rac braid used as 'piping'

Child's dress trimmed in a similar way

● NOTE – ric-rac braid is useful for children's clothes. Of course it is flat but it can look decorative just the same, decorating skirts and dresses made from gingham or brightly coloured plain cottons.

A variation

Another idea though not strictly piping, but used in a similar way, is to substitute shaped insertions instead of piping. These have the added dimension that they can be cut to fit the shape of the seam and so shaped to suit the design.
Begin by measuring the seam. Mark this length on paper and then draw in the shape required. Add seam allowances on all edges and cut out the paper pattern. Using this, cut two pieces of fabric, lay them right sides together and stitch along the shaped free edge only. Clip into corners etc., then turn right side out and press carefully. Stitch the free edges together close to the edge and insert into the seam in the same way you would for piping.

Late 1930s French, printed silk crêpon with contrasting insets on skirt and sleeves

inverted pleats in sleeves held in at top and wrist

1982 Wool crêpe dress trimmed with looped ribbon set onto bias strip set into the yoke

Pattern for inset
add seam allowance
cut a pair from contrasting fabric
Mark to required length and shape
pin with right sides together

stitch shaped edges with small stitches
clip into stitches at angles
trim close to points
(stay stitch angles and points)
turn right side out

1926. Red crêpe de chine, trimmed with white piping, and the whole lot topped with a red felt hat.

Blue silk pyjamas with flat cerise piping

Close fitting jacket with piped seams

light weight cotton crêpe with silky commercial piping

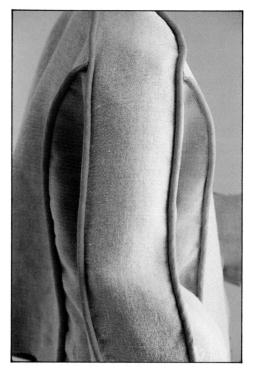

Choose a short loose-fitting jacket pattern with dolman sleeves and a plain round neck (or omit the collar). For the trousers, any shape can be chosen, but they should be very simple, with either patch pockets or pockets set into the side seams (Fig. 1). For the suit illustrated, the jacket front is made to close edge-to-edge, with linked buttons, rather than by overlapping. Side front and side back seams are added and straight bands are set into the shoulders. Pockets are set into the side front seams, though these could easily be omitted. The trousers are made to match the jacket, with a similar piped band set into the side seams and pockets set into the front seams (Figs. 2 and 3). The jacket and trousers can be lined or unlined. If making a lining, use the adapted pattern. The jacket front, only, was lined using the same fabric as the piping.

Fabric

The suit in the photograph was made in a thick, loosely woven linen with the piping and front lining in contrasting and thinner linen, but any soft, supple fabric would be suitable — wool, silk, linen, cotton, or mixtures of these. There are some lovely,

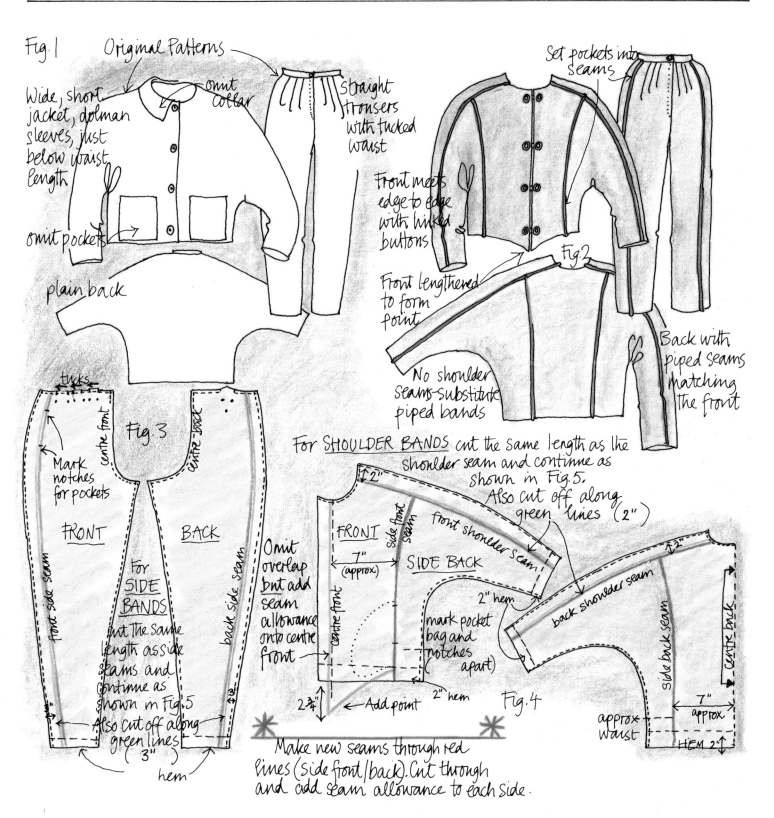

Fig. 1 Original Patterns

Wide, short jacket, dolman sleeves, just below waist Length

omit collar

Straight trousers with tucked waist

omit pockets

plain back

Set pockets into seams

Front meets edge to edge with linked buttons

Front lengthened to form point

Fig. 2

No shoulder seams-substitute piped bands

Back with piped seams matching the front

Fig. 3

tucks

centre front

centre back

Mark notches for pockets

FRONT   BACK

For SIDE BANDS cut the same length as side seams and continue as shown in Fig. 5. Also cut off along green lines (3")

front side seam

back side seam

hem

For SHOULDER BANDS cut the same length as the shoulder seam and continue as shown in Fig. 5. Also cut off along green lines (2")

Omit overlap but add seam allowance onto centre front

FRONT

2"

7" (approx.)

side front seam

front shoulder seam

SIDE BACK

2" hem

centre front

mark pocket bag and notches apart)

2" hem

2¾"

←Add point

Fig. 4

2"

back shoulder seam

side back seam

centre back

approx waist

7" approx.

HEM 2"

Make new seams through red lines (side front/back). Cut through and add seam allowance to each side.

inexpensive thick cotton and silky tweed Indian fabrics available, and these too would be ideal, as would any of the softer Scottish or Irish tweeds. If you are going to wash the suit, do make sure that the fabric (and piping cord) you choose is washable before buying it. If you are still not sure, wash a small sample before beginning the project. If it looks good afterwards, but has shrunk, wash the whole length before cutting out the pattern.

● REMEMBER – to check whether the piping cord is pre-shrunk – it usually is, otherwise the advice on washing and pre-shrinking will apply to the cord too, but bind the ends first to stop it unravelling.

Altering the basic pattern

Alter the front and back of the jacket as shown in Fig. 4 and the trousers as in Fig. 3. Draw up patterns for shoulder and leg bands as Fig. 5. When all these alterations have been transferred to your pattern, cut out the main pieces from the fabric and also the lining fabric, if it is to be lined. If the jacket is not to be lined cut the front double (i.e. two pairs of fronts) and a back neck facing using either the main fabric or that used for the piping.

For a lined jacket cut out in the main fabric and piping fabric:
1 pair fronts
1 back
1 pair shoulder bands
1 pair side backs
1 pair side fronts
2 pairs pocket bags in piping fabric only

For an unlined jacket cut out as above in main fabric, plus one pair fronts in piping fabric and a bias strip to face the back neck.

For trousers cut out in main fabric:
1 pair fronts
1 pair backs
1 pair side bands
1 waistband
Also cut enough bias strips for all the piping, see page 39.
Make up the piping.

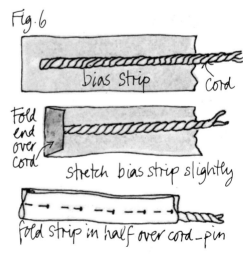

Experiment with different gauges of piping cord. It is probably best to make up samples of the seams, each with a different gauge of piping. Decide on

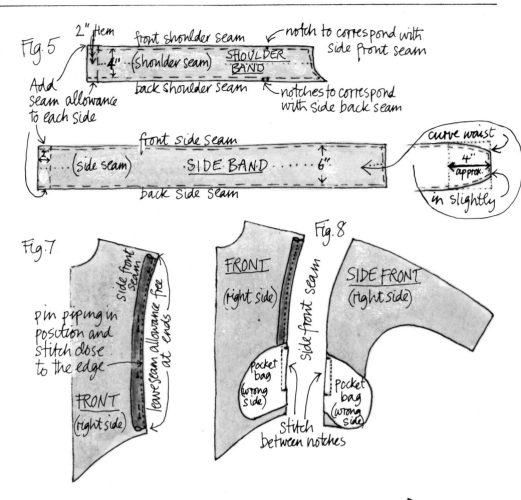

the gauge you like best, then cut enough bias strips for all the piping, referring back to page 39 for details. However, since in the sample the ends do not run into the seams in the usual way, finish them with a new method: cut the bias strip 1in. longer at each end than the piping and then use the extra to wrap neatly around the cut ends of the cord before stitching (Fig. 6).

● REMEMBER – keep the seam allowance on the piping the same as that on the seams to be piped.

Making up the suit

Make up the suit in the order given:

The jacket front Make up two pieces of piping for the fronts to run from the sewing line at the shoulder, down the side front seam to the fold line of the hem. Pin the piping in position and stitch close to the cut edges (Fig. 7). Pin the relevant pocket bags in place, right sides together (over the piping)

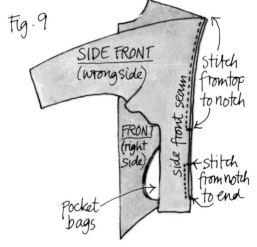

matching notches on fronts and side fronts. Stitch close to the cord between the pocket notches on front and side fronts (Fig. 8). Pin the side fronts in position on the fronts, right sides together, over the piping and pocket bag. Stitch close to the cord, from the top of the side front seam to the top pocket notch and from the lower pocket notch to the end (Fig. 9). Push

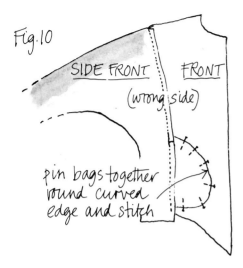

Fig. 10

SIDE FRONT   FRONT

(wrong side)

pin bags together round curved edge and stitch

bags through to wrong side. Pin and stitch round the curved edge of the pocket bags from notch to notch. Fold and press the bag and seams to lie under the front and clip into the seam allowance at the corners where necessary (Fig. 10).

Back Make up the piping and stitch in place on the side back seams. Pin the side backs in place at the side back seams, right sides together and over the piping. Stitch from the top to the lower edge. Press seams under back close to the cord.

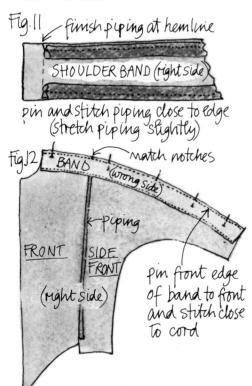

Fig. 11 finish piping at hemline

SHOULDER BAND (right side)

pin and stitch piping close to edge (stretch piping slightly)

Fig. 12 match notches

BAND (wrong side)

FRONT   SIDE FRONT

(right side)

piping

pin front edge of band to front and stitch close to cord

Variations:—

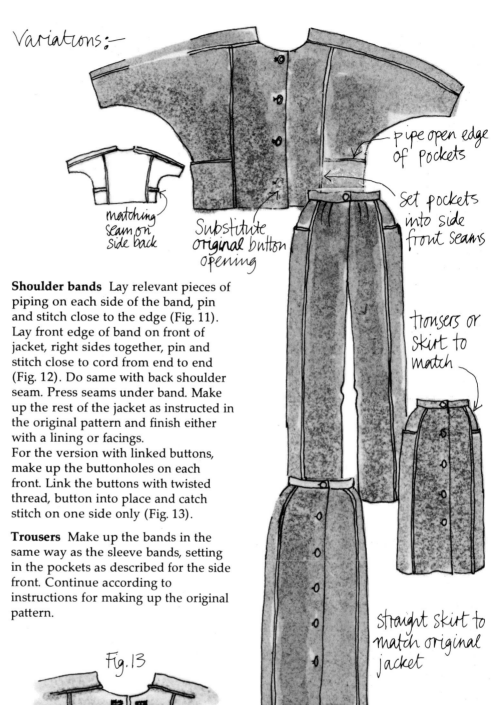

matching seam on side back

Substitute original button opening

pipe open edge of pockets

Set pockets into side front seams

trousers or skirt to match

straight skirt to match original jacket

Shoulder bands Lay relevant pieces of piping on each side of the band, pin and stitch close to the edge (Fig. 11). Lay front edge of band on front of jacket, right sides together, pin and stitch close to cord from end to end (Fig. 12). Do same with back shoulder seam. Press seams under band. Make up the rest of the jacket as instructed in the original pattern and finish either with a lining or facings.

For the version with linked buttons, make up the buttonholes on each front. Link the buttons with twisted thread, button into place and catch stitch on one side only (Fig. 13).

Trousers Make up the bands in the same way as the sleeve bands, setting in the pockets as described for the side front. Continue according to instructions for making up the original pattern.

Fig. 13

make buttonholes opposite each other

link buttons with thread

Variations

The jacket could be made with the original front fastening shown in the pattern. The linked button motif could be omitted altogether on the sleeves and at the ankles, or be made to overlap to match the front. A thinner piping cord could be substituted for the very thick cord used for the sample.

Topstitching

Ignore this technique at your peril.
It is, besides being decorative, an integral part of dressmaking and therefore
a technique unlike any of the others in the book, which are solely embellishments.
It constitutes a passport to more professional dressmaking because it improves the finish of a garment.
Look at current ready-made clothes and you will find that many of them have seams
and edges decorated with one or two lines of topstitching;
these hold the fabric flat, giving a finished look that is rarely seen in a beginner's work.
So read on and find out how to improve and decorate your dressmaking at one and the same time.

◄ *This sampler shows how easily and effectively topstitching can be used for*
'drawing' quite detailed pictures.

White blouse decorated with chevrons of blue topstitching

Top stitched facings

Pleat held with topstitching

Fabric

Topstitching may be used on almost any fabric, from the thin and stiff to the thick and soft – use it:
a) to hold the shape on voiles and lawns
b) to give crispness to crêpes
c) to keep edges sharp on poplins or piqués
d) to flatten seams on soft, heavy linens and cottons
e) to give weight and swing to airy mohairs or on almost any fabric as decoration.

● BEWARE – of twilled (diagonal) weaves which tend to wiggle about in a most unbecoming way if topstitched.

Richly textured fabrics are probably the main group which do not, generally, topstitch well, as the stitches might be hidden by the texture or it may be difficult, because of a rough surface, say, to stitch a smooth line. But do experiment on unlikely fabrics if you feel it would give a better finish to a garment, as surprisingly interesting effects can sometimes appear.

Amateur dressmakers tend to avoid topstitching mistakenly thinking that it is too difficult, because they feel they are unable to sew straight enough. The best way to overcome this problem is to examine the topstitching on bought clothes which may look convincing at first glance; a closer look often reveals that the lines are not absolutely straight. It is the impression that counts; no-one is going to pick over the clothes you are wearing and tell you that the topstitching is not straight. Do not worry – just do it.
Practice means improvement, so keep at it and you will soon be sewing passable topstitching.

● AVOID – studying 'haute couture' when looking through finished clothes for morale boosting purposes. Their topstitching should be perfect, and might well make the aspiring topstitcher feel inadequate!

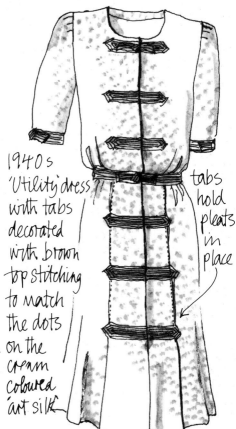

1940s 'Utility' dress with tabs decorated with brown topstitching to match the dots on the cream coloured 'art silk'

tabs hold pleats in place

1930s

Black stitching on cream silk

1930s Thick grey silk thread conched with black zigzag on pale grey silk

The technique can also be used to create a linking motif on different fabrics, for example a black suit with a white blouse topstitched in black, or the same motif worked on two different coloured fabrics to give a co-ordinated effect.
Striped fabrics can sometimes be topstitched with interesting results, and the occasional patterned fabric can be topstitched to accent a colour in the pattern. As usual, experiment is the key to new designs. Look at every fabric with an eye open to inspiration but do not expect every experiment to yield useful results.

● EXPERIMENT – with lots of topstitching to transform a dreary or mundane fabric into something more interesting.

Picture libraries and archives are full of pictures like the one on the left; unidentified women of the past modelling the clothes of their period. This elegant creation is simple in outline, with all the emphasis placed at the neck with a topstitched jabot. An easy enough idea, and so easy to do.

Whereas the photograph on the left is probably from the 1930s, the illustration above, from the magazine 'L'Art et La Mode', most certainly is! The fashions are dateable by their long lean lines and the accessories, as well as the style of drawing.

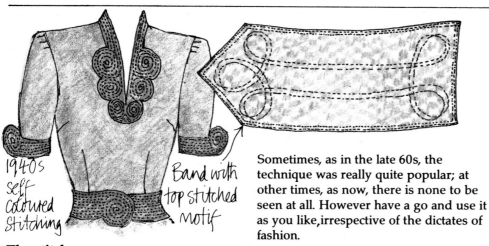

1940s self coloured stitching

Band with top stitched motif

The stitches

There are two basic stitches to use, straight machine stitch and zigzag. (Hand-sewn topstitching is not included here.)

Straight stitch This is the most widely used, and combined with different stitch lengths, colour, texture and fabric, is extremely versatile.

Zigzag stitch This can also be used in a variety of stitch sizes, from a wide zigzag giving a satin stitch to a small open zigzag. Again a choice of colour, texture and thickness of thread all help to give diversity and, added to the texture and colour of the fabric, a wide assortment of decorative effects can be achieved. Although straight topstitching can be said to go on forever, the fashion for zigzag seems to come and go.

Sometimes, as in the late 60s, the technique was really quite popular; at other times, as now, there is none to be seen at all. However have a go and use it as you like, irrespective of the dictates of fashion.

The thread

Most topstitching is done with the thread used to make up the garment; sometimes a slightly thicker thread of the same colour is substituted. A more decorative effect can be achieved by choosing a different tone or contrasting colour which helps to reveal your hard work for all to see. Indigo blue dyed clothes from many countries are often decorated with white topstitching on seams and edges, and sometimes also incorporate interesting motifs.

Thicker threads can be used to emphasise the stitches but may need to be wound onto the bobbin of the machine (see your sewing machine manual).

For a luscious look, use lots of flossy embroidery thread, both for straight and zigzag topstitching.

Machine embroidery threads, which give a smoother shinier finish than most ordinary machine threads, can sometimes be found in the larger haberdashery departments. Pure silk threads are available for both hand and machine work, and even those for the former can sometimes be cajoled into giving a 'lift' to rough or dull textured fabrics, again by using the bobbin and 'topstitching' from the wrong side. Thin threads can be used to couch thicker ones in place with zigzag stitches.

Finally, remember that there is no reason why two or more colours should not be combined on a fabric of another colour, thus turning an ordinary fabric into an interesting garment.

Designing with topstitching

Many clothes just do not look finished without topstitching. Burberrys and other raincoats of the same type rely on rows of topstitching on collars, revers, belts, yokes, pockets, tabs and most of the seams. Tweed coats and suits are often finished in this way but remember that the techniques used must be thought about from the inception of the design; it is no good suddenly thinking, half way through making up the garment, "Oh let's finish this with topstitching!" Too late. Your seam allowance may well be so narrow that the stitching will miss it completely.

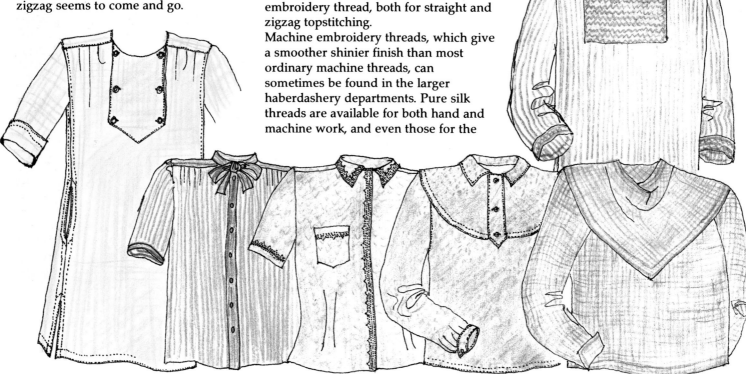

From French 'Elle' magazine, by Helmut Newton.
Does the interesting topstitching on these 60s
mini dresses add to the surreal quality of the
photograph?

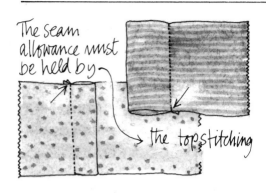

The seam allowance must be held by → the topstitching

● PLAN AHEAD – work out your design, then decide how to put the garment together – which seams will be topstitched and how close to the seam the stitching lines should be so that you can allow for a suitable seam allowance. Relating the topstitching from one part of the garment to another is the next point to bear in mind. Obviously you will use the same thread over the whole garment but you might also like to think about reflecting a double row of topstitching used on say a yoke, to that used to hold the hem, which should, logically, be stitched in the same way.

Working topstitching

First of all, give yourself a chance. This may sound obvious, but I have often seen students trying to stitch multiple

1960s Dark green velveteen with matching zig-zag decoration

On stretchy fabrics a backing fabric can be used under motifs to keep the shape

rows on an almost finished garment. This is a hopeless task as the bulk of the garment gets in the way.

THINK – first! Topstitch each part as soon as possible in the making up sequence. For example, a collar can usually be topstitched before attaching it to the neck; however, if the stitching is to continue onto the rever, you will need to attach the collar first, but topstitch before making the side seams. In other words, use your head, and keep everything as small, open and flat as possible.

● REMEMBER – as unpressed seams and edges are rounded, they are impossible to topstitch satisfactorily and must always be pressed, perfectly, first. Tacking is unnecessary; it is just as easy – if not easier – to machine straight as it is to tack straight, and so a delusion to think that a line of tacking will help. If you machine over tacking you will also have the horrid job of picking out all the odd little bits of tacking thread, and this process sometimes pulls the machine stitches. Make up your mind that you are going to sew straight and at a given distance from the seam or edge, but do not expect perfection at first. Try a few practice rows first, both to decide which thread to use and the most suitable length of stitch.

● AVOID – very small stitches which tend to produce a stiff line of topstitching, especially if you plan to work several rows close together.

● REMEMBER – that multiple rows of stitching also tend to stiffen the seam. However there may be occasions when this is an advantage.

● REMEMBER – it is easier, as in all machining, to stitch a short distance at a time.

● EXPERIMENT – with different combinations of stitch length and thread until you achieve an effect you like.

● EXPERIMENT – with which layers of fabric are going to be included in the topstitching. For instance, on a collar the stitching can be worked on the single top layer before it is made up, or on a double layer after the interlining has been attached, or through three layers after the collar has been made up. Each method will give a slightly different effect.

Judging the width for the stitching

Use the presser foot of the machine as a guide – the zigzag foot, being wider, is useful when the ordinary foot is too narrow. Alternatively, hang a tape measure round your neck and hold one end on the seam or edge to use as a guide as you go; though after a few inches you will be able to judge the width accurately and so be able to dispense with the tape measure. Select easy fabrics to start on, avoiding anything slippery or stretchy until you are more confident.

For multiple rows of topstitching the presser foot is usually the best guide as the rows are invariably close together. Some machines have calibrations marked on the needle plate and these are useful for edges, though not much help on seams.

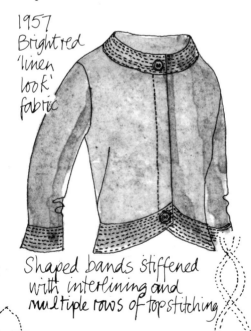

1957 Bright red 'linen look' fabric

Shaped bands stiffened with interlining and multiple rows of topstitching

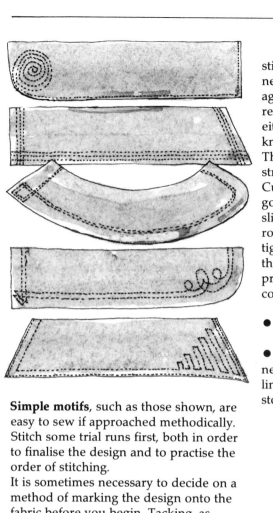

Blue and white ticking with red top-stitching

white velour hat covered in topstitching

Cotton hat stiffened with topstitching

Black velvet with white stitching

Black + white stripes with red stitching

stitch to the next corner, leave the needle in the fabric, then lift and turn again. Continue in this way until you reach the centre of the motif, finishing either with a few back stitches or by knotting the ends on the wrong side. These instructions can be adapted for all straight-sided motifs.

Curved motifs need a steady hand and a good eye. Loosen the presser foot slightly so that you can pull the fabric round slightly as you go. For even tighter curves, it will be necessary to lift the foot slightly as you stitch, which with practice is not too difficult, but is of course slow.

● DO – give yourself lots of time.

● DO – design motifs which run as nearly as possible in one continuous line; this will avoid too many starts and stops.

Simple motifs, such as those shown, are easy to sew if approached methodically. Stitch some trial runs first, both in order to finalise the design and to practise the order of stitching.

It is sometimes necessary to decide on a method of marking the design onto the fabric before you begin. Tacking, as mentioned before, is usually unsatisfactory; chalk pounded through holes punched at intervals is a better method, though sometimes soft pencil dots can be substituted, depending on the fabric being used. Patent marking papers and pens are usually best avoided.

To stitch a motif similar to the one shown below, start at the outside of the triangle and stitch the first side to the corner, leaving the needle in the fabric. Lift the presser foot, turn the fabric until you are in line to stitch the second side,

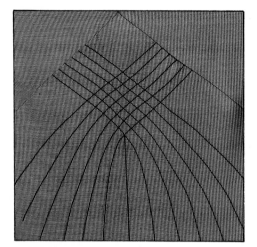

Boiler suits made of silk seem to be a contradiction in terms, but few boiler suits are worn today for tending boilers, an accepted anachronism, so perhaps this further aberration is another step in the right direction, adding a touch of luxury to inconsistency.

Choose a loose fitting pattern with no waist seam, but with deep armholes and wide sleeves. The revers will probably need to be enlarged, thus allowing the crossed rows of topstitching to show up really well.

The pattern will also need to be adapted to include yokes on front and back, where the topstitching detail from the revers is repeated but flared out to form a motif. The sleeves have been curved and pockets inserted in the side seams; both are optional adaptations. The belt is made from the diagram given on page 59.

Size

This entirely depends on the size of pattern you use. The few measurements that are given are approximate, but should cover sizes 8–14 quite adequately.

Fabric

Choose a strongly woven fabric, avoiding anything stiff. It will make up the same as a similar weight cotton or linen and, of course, one of these fabrics could be substituted if preferred. If you like the idea of using silk, look for names such as Honan, Shantung or Spunsilk – just three of the many different types of silk fabric, which will probably be about the same price as a good quality cotton.

Although silk is an unusual fabric to use, it is perfectly practical as long as it is washable. Most shops will tell you that silk can only be dry-cleaned; this is rarely true, however, so be persistent in your questioning and don't take any such claim at face value.

Note: it is a good idea to wash the fabric before cutting out and making up in case it shrinks. This is as true for silk as any other fabric, but test on a scrap first. If it does not wash well, dry-clean the fabric or choose another to work with instead. If you are planning to use lining and interlining, wash these too.

Thread

Use a matching thread for making up and a slightly thicker contrasting thread for the topstitching.

Adapting the basic pattern

There are two ways you can make this outfit, either by using a basic pattern for a boiler suit, or by combining a jacket or shirt with a pair of trousers. First, using a suit pattern (Fig. 1):

Front yoke Mark the yoke on the front pattern (Fig. 2). Lay the pattern on a piece of folded paper; draw round it and

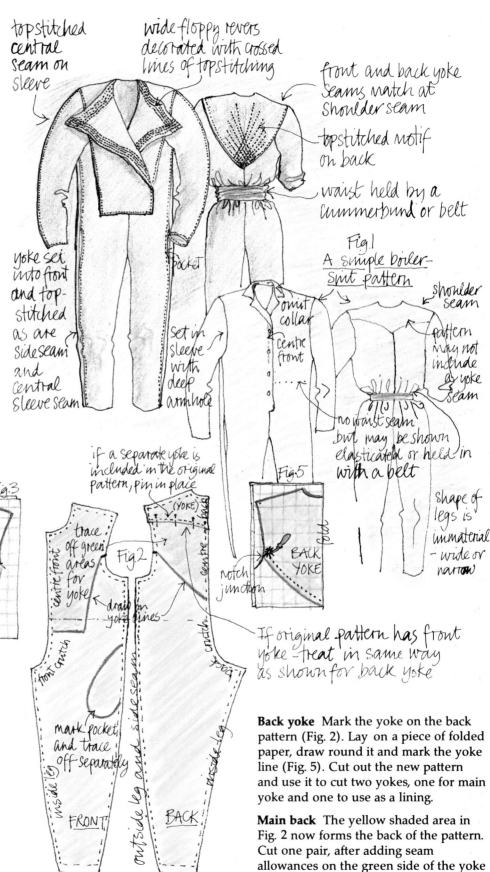

topstitched central seam on sleeve

wide floppy revers decorated with crossed lines of topstitching

front and back yoke seams match at shoulder seam

topstitched motif on back

waist held by a cummerbund or belt

Fig. 1
A simple boiler-suit pattern

yoke set into front and top-stitched as are side seam and central sleeve seam

Pocket

omit collar

centre front

Set in sleeve with deep armhole

shoulder seam

pattern may not include a yoke seam

no waist seam but may be shown elasticated or held in with a belt

Fig. 5

shape of legs is immaterial - wide or narrow

if a separate yoke is included in the original pattern, pin in place

trace off green areas for yoke

(YOKE)

centre front

draw in yoke lines

Fig. 2

centre front

BACK YOKE

notch junction

If original pattern has front yoke-treat in same way as shown for back yoke

front crutch

mark pocket and trace off separately

inside leg

FRONT

outside leg and side seam

crutch

back leg

inside leg

BACK

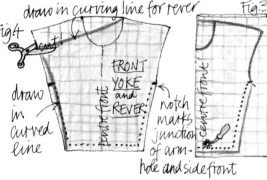

draw in curving line for rever

Fig. 3

Fig. 4

front

draw in curved line

FRONT YOKE and REVER

notch marks junction of arm-hole and side front

centre front

mark the yoke line. Cut out except around the neck (Fig. 3). Open the yoke out (Fig. 4). Mark a line for the top edge of the rever as shown and cut through to complete the yoke pattern and use it to cut two pairs from fabric, one to make into the left front together with its facing, the other the right front and its facing.

Main front The yellow shaded part of the pattern shown in Fig. 2 forms the side bodice and trouser front. Cut out one pair, after adding seam allowances on the green side of the yoke seam.

Back yoke Mark the yoke on the back pattern (Fig. 2). Lay on a piece of folded paper, draw round it and mark the yoke line (Fig. 5). Cut out the new pattern and use it to cut two yokes, one for main yoke and one to use as a lining.

Main back The yellow shaded area in Fig. 2 now forms the back of the pattern. Cut one pair, after adding seam allowances on the green side of the yoke seam.

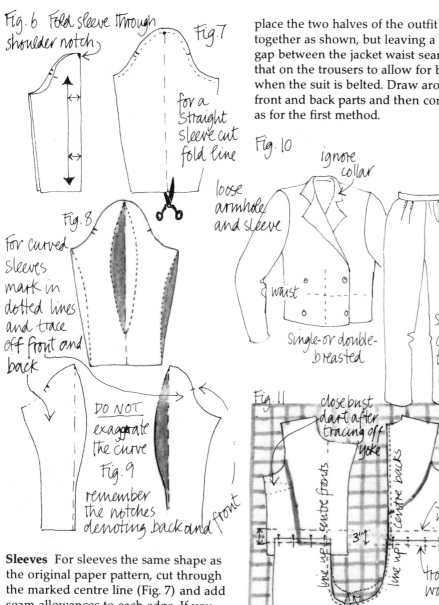

Fig. 6 Fold sleeve through shoulder notch

Fig. 7 for a straight sleeve cut fold line

Fig. 8 For curved sleeves mark in dotted lines and trace off front and back

DO NOT exaggerate the curve

Fig. 9 remember the notches denoting back and front

Sleeves For sleeves the same shape as the original paper pattern, cut through the marked centre line (Fig. 7) and add seam allowances to each edge. If you want a curved shape similar to the sample shown at the beginning of the project, trace off the front sleeve (Fig. 8), adding on the curved segment shaded grey at the centre of the sleeve and subtracting the curved segment shown, shaded grey, on the inside of the underarm (Fig. 7). Do the same for the back part of the sleeve.

For either version – cut one pair of front sleeves and one pair of back sleeves.

● ALTERNATIVELY – combine two patterns to make one. Choose a single-or double-breasted jacket pattern and a pair of simple drawstring style trousers, or other loosely fitted trousers with straight or tapered legs. Using Fig. 10 as a guide,

Fig. 10 ignore collar / loose armhole and sleeve / waist / single- or double-breasted / straight or tapered legs

Fig. 11 close bust dart after tracing off yoke / line up centre fronts / line up centre backs / jacket waist / trouser waist / 3" / raise crutch 2" to ensure that it will not be too low. Cut away after first fitting if necessary

place the two halves of the outfit together as shown, but leaving a 3in. gap between the jacket waist seam and that on the trousers to allow for blousing when the suit is belted. Draw around the front and back parts and then continue as for the first method.

Of course, you could use a boiler suit pattern with a waist seam and adapt it in a similar way (Figs. 10 and 11.)

Making up a toile

Make up a toile first if you feel unsure about these alterations. This will allow you to make all necessary adjustments and get the pattern right before cutting into your precious silk. It is not necessary however to make up the full length of the legs as the changes are to the top and sleeves. Make up both sleeves; if one only is made it can easily pull to one side without being noticed. Machine rather than tack the toile, using a very large stitch – it is much quicker.

Making up the suit

Follow the instructions for the original pattern as far as possible but in the order given below:

Topstitching yoke and revers This will tend to stiffen the fabric, so if a soft look is wanted, as exemplified in the sample, it would be best to topstitch the revers and back yoke before making up the whole garment (Fig. 12). If using a very thick thread for topstitching, it may be easier to wind this onto the bobbin (the underneath thread) and use a thinner thread on the top to topstitch from the wrong side. This has the great advantage that the first line to be stitched can be marked on the wrong side of the fabric with a soft pencil, so making it easier to see exactly where to stitch. The second and subsequent lines can be stitched using the previous line and the presser foot as a guide.

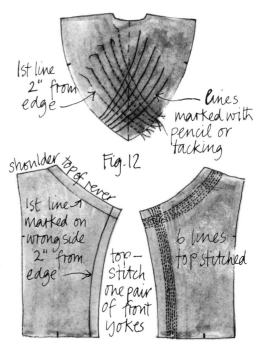

Fig. 12 1st line 2" from edge / lines marked with pencil or tacking / shoulder top of rever / 1st line marked on wrong side 2" from edge / topstitch one pair of front yokes / 6 lines topstitched

58

- DO – practise topstitching on spare pieces of fabric.

- DO – try out the stitch length. It should be long enough not to stiffen the fabric but short enough to make a good stitch.

Note: The sample fabric used had a slightly ridged surface on the right side – another good reason for topstitching from the wrong side.

Set on the yoke and revers

If interlining is needed, attach to the topstitched pieces at this point (none was used in the sample). Join the topstitched pair of fronts to the back yoke lining at the shoulder seam; do the same with the other pair of fronts, attaching them to the topstitched back yoke but pressing the seam under the yoke.

Press the seam allowances under the back. Place these two pieces right sides together, pin and stitch the neck, across the top of the revers, turn the corner and continue to the lower edge. Clip curved edges (Fig. 13). Press.

Fig. 16

right yoke overlaps left yoke

Start top stitching from lower end of left front

stitch back yoke in direction of arrows

Front and back Clip into the corners of the main front pieces to the seam line (Fig. 14) after stay stitching. Sew the crutch seams on the back; stitch to the seam line, at the waist – i.e. not to the cut edge (Fig. 15). Stitch the side seams, setting in the pockets. Press seam allowance under front and topstitch. Stitch the inside leg seam.

Sleeves Make the centre seams. Press the seam allowances under the back and topstitch. Make the underarm seams.

Set on the sleeves Pin and stitch lower part of armhole, matching underarm to side seam. Press seam allowance under sleeve.

Set on the yoke (See Fig. 16). Stitch the (topstitched) back yoke to the back. This is easiest if done in two parts, first one side then the other, stitching each from notch for armhole on yoke to point. Pin sleeves in place on yoke, matching shoulder seams and continue pinning side fronts to (untopstitched) yoke fronts and on right front only, turn at the corner and continue across the lower edge to the front edge. Stitch. Press seam allowance under yoke.

Finishing the yoke Working with the garment inside out: press the seam allowances to the wrong side on the free edges of the yoke lining, except the lower front edges, clipping into the seam allowances, so that they will lie flat. On the lower edge of the left front, pin and stitch the two free edges together, keeping them flat. Lay in position on top

of the right front, then pin and stitch and neaten raw edges together. Pin and tack the yoke lining in position. Turn the garment right side out and topstitch all round yoke, starting at the lower edge of the left front (Fig. 16). Mark and make buttonholes and sew on buttons to correspond. Turn up the hems at the wrist and ankles.

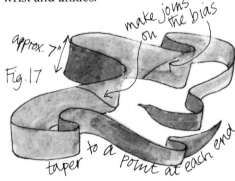

make joins on the bias

approx. 7"

Fig. 17

taper to a point at each end

Belt Cut a piece of fabric on the bias, joining as necessary to make up a sufficient length to fit twice around your waist and tie a knot (Fig. 17).

Other ideas

Instead of topstitching, the suit illustrated could be trimmed with piping perhaps using a contrasting colour. Alternatively the yoke seams could be bound, using a striped or patterned contrast, or make up the whole suit in a striped fabric. For all these techniques, turn to the relevant chapters.

Finally, if you do not want a boiler suit but would like a topstitched outfit, why not adapt the instructions given here to make a jacket and skirt or trousers?

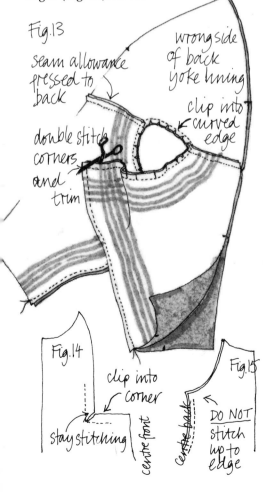

Fig. 13

seam allowance pressed to back

wrong side of back yoke lining

clip into curved edge

double stitch corners and trim

Fig. 14

clip into corner

stay stitching

centre front

Fig. 15

centre back

DO NOT stitch up to edge

Pintucks

Pintucks are just that: tucks as wide as a pin.
They are usually straight and stitched in groups that run vertically or horizontally;
often worked in conjunction with lace or broderie anglaise insertions.
They can also be used to 'draw' pictures, as in the sampler opposite, or to make
striped effects or repeating patterns to decorate plain fabrics.
In the days of cheap labour, blouses, camisoles and underclothes were often encrusted with pintucks.
A dedicated dressmaker might spend hours pintucking allover patterns and borders which,
whilst dazzling the onlooker, would undoubtedly bankrupt her clients!
By the 20s they were used more frugally though more interestingly
but it was in the 30s that they were used most successfully, often as part of the structure of a garment,
giving subtle shapes to dresses, costumes and lightweight suits.
Pintucks began to curve, to cross each other and negotiate corners,
which allowed more scope for their use and helped to cut down
on the number needed to make an impression, or become,
a feature of the design of the whole garment.

◄ *An example of how a dressmaking technique can be used pictorially.*
Stitch a gallery of silhouettes in pintucked outline.

Pintucks look so intricate that they might be thought difficult to sew, but this is simply not the case; given an organised approach and some practice, they are really quite easy. The first point to notice, is that even on quite expensive garments, pintucks are rarely absolutely perfect; it is the group impression that counts, or their effect from a distance. Sometimes one pintuck might wiggle about, the next slightly less so, then the third be quite straight. But as long as the outer pintucks in a group are straight, the eye will be deceived into thinking it is seeing the whole group as straight.

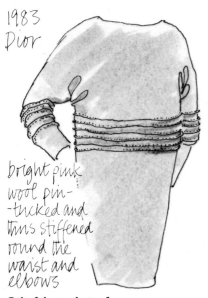

1983 Dior

bright pink wool pin- -tucked and thus stiffened round the waist and elbows

Stitching pintucks

To practise, fold a sample piece of fabric, wrong sides together, and backstitch two or three stitches very close to the folded edge. Hold the fold, with the right hand between 3–4in. away from the needle and stitch, keeping close to the edge. Re-position the hands to hold the fold another 3–4in. away from the needle and stitch again. Continue stitching short lengths in this way to the end of the pintuck.

● AVOID – using too small a stitch as this may stiffen the pintuck.

● EXPERIMENT – with how far from the edge to sew. This will vary according to the fabric, but normally 1/16in. is about right. If the pintucks are too wide they will look clumsy; if they are too narrow they will not form a tuck, just a

1965

Chanel navy wool and red silk

← pintucks →

ridge. They should be wide enough to just fold to one side, lying more or less flat when pressed.

● BEWARE – some sewing machines claim to make pintucks automatically, with a special foot or needle being provided. These are not real pintucks, however, just ridges made by nipping the fabric together, usually using a twin needle. They may be useful but will not be the genuine article and no easier to sew straight than real pintucks.

Pressing pintucks

This is always done from the wrong side. Use a spray, or a damp cloth for woollen fabrics. Use the point of the iron, pushing it along the pintucks and turning them so that they all face in the same direction.

Thread

Pintucks are almost invariably stitched with the same thread as that used to make up the garment. It might be interesting, however, to experiment with contrasting colours when sewing pintucks for motifs or pictures. The sampler shown at the beginning of this chapter, for example, was stitched using a slightly darker tone of thread than the colour of the fabric in order to accentuate the pintucks.

● AVOID – using too thick a thread as this may make the stitching bulky.

Marking pintucks

It is generally only necessary to mark one end of the first pintuck in a group of

pintucks. Usually a pin, notch or chalk mark will be enough.

For more complicated pintucks – the 'V' on the back of the jacket in the project shown on page 68, for instance – one pintuck can be marked as a guide for all. Use chalk and measure it out with a tape measure. If the chalk will not hold on the surface of the fabric effectively, the line can be tacked.

On the sampler shown at the beginning, the design was drawn out on paper, holes were punched along the lines, transferred using chalk onto the fabric, and then tacked with a contrasting thread. On work of this sort, absolute accuracy is essential, as the expression on the face relies on the exact curve of the lip, nose etc., and even a minute variation may alter a serene expression to a sneer or grimace.

(I found it necessary to practise marking and stitching several times to get this just right.)

Working groups of pintucks

Make one pintuck near the left of the piece of fabric and open out the material.

Refold the fabric about 3/8in. to the right and stitch a second pintuck. Notice where the presser foot lies in relation to the first pintuck.

Open out the material and then fold again, using your eyes and the presser foot as guides to keep the width between the first and second pintuck the same.

Stitch a third pintuck in the same way and continue until they are all complete. Press.

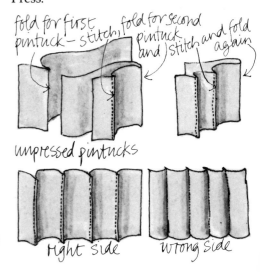

fold for first pintuck – stitch; fold for second pintuck and stitch and fold again

unpressed pintucks

right side   wrong side

- DO – judge the width by eye right from the start. A tape measure is more of a hindrance than a help; it slows the work down if you keep stopping to measure and you will learn to judge the width surprisingly quickly.

- DO – work from left to right to avoid having great wodges of fabric stuck under the machine.

- DO – where possible, use the straight grain of the fabric as a guide to help keep the pintucks and stitching straight.

- AVOID – stitching down one pintuck and then up the next, as this tends to distort the fabric. Work a group starting always from one end. (I tend to work pintucks from top to bottom, i.e. from the shoulder to hem, although this is not always possible.) Generally it pays to be systematic!

Crossed pintucks

These are much easier than they look. Mark out your design first as shown and then work one group one way before pressing them firmly. Stitch the next group and press these too. You will find there is no problem with the actual crossing if the first group are thoroughly pressed before starting on the second or 'crossing' group. And that is all there is to it. Nothing too difficult, and you will amaze your friends with the dazzling displays of crossed pintucks with which you can decorate your clothes.

Fancy or random pintucks

These present only one real problem, and that is coping with the variation of the grain in the fabric. In some places the pintuck will run along the warp, in others along the weft, and also at any angle to either. This means that the pintuck will tend to stretch in some places and not in others; so take great care, especially when sewing at an angle to the grain.

Wavy and random pintucks will usually need to be marked with chalk or tacking to produce an accurate result.

The fabric used should be soft and supple, crêpes being the best group from which to choose, both to avoid stiffness and because they can be pressed back into shape more successfully than most fabrics. Mark one pintuck from a group and stitch. Use the forefinger, held tightly behind the presser foot, on the bias parts to help stop any stretching.

Use the first pintuck as a guide, as before, to stitch the rest of the group. If the pintucks are to cross, press the first group before stitching the second.

Zigzags and pintucks with points

These obviously rely on the points being neatly stitched. This is fairly slow to do, so keep the points down to a reasonable number especially if you don't have a lot of time, or patience!

Fold the first angle and stitch up to the first point, leaving the needle in the fabric. (Take great care not to stretch the fabric as the stitching will usually be on the cross.)

Lift the presser foot up, fold the fabric for the second angle, pulling it round to be in line for stitching. Lower the presser foot and stitch to the next point. Continue in this way to the end.

Press this first pintuck and use it as a guide for the second if working a group. Work this in exactly the same way.

Where these more complicated pintucks cross themselves, it is impossible to press before the crossing pintuck is stitched, so great care must be taken to hold the first pintuck flat whilst stitching over it, using the point of your sewing scissors if necessary. Practice is the only way to get good results with complex pintucking such as this.

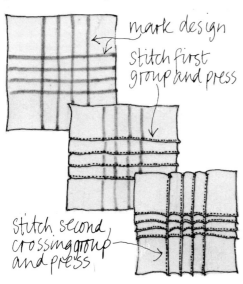

mark design

stitch first group and press

stitch second crossing group and press

mark with chalk and tack if necessary

stitch first group and press

stitch second group and press

wavy pintucks stitched with darker thread

Designing with pintucks

Pintucks can be used in two basic ways:
1. **As decoration** – for this the pintuck can either be sewn across a piece of fabric, or the pintucks used to form motifs or designs.
2. **As a way of holding fullness** – an even more interesting use, as the pintucks become part of the structure of the garment. The fullness is taken up in the pintucks, so cutting down on bulk and giving a smoother outline. On pieces that are to have a lot of pintucks, or for motifs, it is usually easiest to pintuck the fabric before cutting out the pattern pieces. Cut out a piece roughly to the shape of the finished pattern, but make it larger.

If using fullness already available, such as where gathers or a dart is marked, work short pintucks to contain the fullness which will be released at the end of each tuck.

Yokes and bands can be pintucked to hold fullness, releasing it at the edge. To do this, however, the yoke must be cut in one with the main bodice. Work out how many tucks will be needed to take up the extra length added to the yoke; then stitch this number from the shoulder down to the required length.

Allowing for pintucks

Extra fabric should be allowed exactly where the pintucks are required, or should be added to the nearest edge. Start by marking their position on the pattern as shown. Then either:
a) cut through the centre of the group and spread the pattern pieces apart by the necessary amount on another piece of paper, and stick them in place. This applies to pieces where the pintucking is not near an edge.
b) add the extra onto the nearest straight edge. This applies especially to square or rectangular pieces, but also if the band of pintucks is near a straight edge.

Design motifs so that they are easy to sew. This one is formed from one continuous line

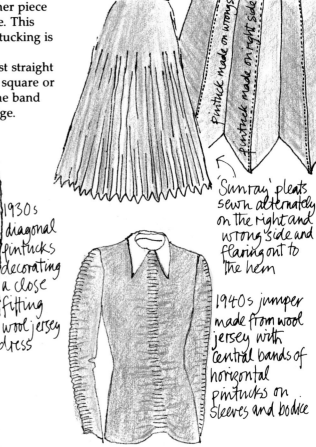

'Sunray' pleats sewn alternately on the right and wrong side and flaring out to the hem

1940s jumper made from wool jersey with central bands of horizontal pintucks on sleeves and bodice

1930s diagonal pintucks decorating a close fitting wool jersey dress

pintucked yoke on flared skirt

1965 Chanel pintucks give fluted effect on thick tweed

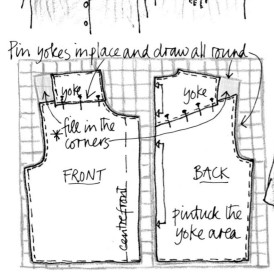

yoke seam   shoulder seams   yoke seam

Use a pattern for a blouse like this to make a pintucked yoke like this

Pin yokes in place and draw all round

yoke

yoke

fill in the corners

FRONT   BACK

centre front

pintuck the yoke area

A classic pintucks and lawn blouse.

Pintucks running into a seam look a bit bald – why not dispense with the seam? perhaps grade the ends to form a point

Yokes can be pintucked parallel to their edges

Estimating yardage

Pintucks take up so little fabric that they make little difference to the overall amount of fabric required. However, the pieces of the pattern may need to be spread out a little when laying them out on the fabric, so work out the layout in advance to allow for this.

Suitable fabrics

Fine cotton or linen fabrics are often used for pintucks, but lightweight silks and wools are also suitable.
The jacket and skirt given as the project at the end of this chapter are made in a fine wool crêpe which is ideal for

pintucking. Softness and pliability are the characteristics to look for; in other words, go for a material that will not stiffen after stitching or distort after pressing, especially if you plan to stitch motifs or complicated pintucked designs. In the 1940s and 50s, blouse fronts, made from the new transparent nylon fabrics, were often closely pintucked, thus making them more modest and wearable.

● EXPERIMENT – with different weights and textures. Try thicker fabrics (even tweeds have sometimes been pintucked effectively).

● EXPERIMENT – with pintucks on furnishing fabrics to make interesting textures and patterns for cushions.

● REMEMBER – that some fabrics are woven using a thicker warp than weft, or vice versa and that this will affect the pintucks; they may look different if sewn across the fabric rather than parallel to the selvedge. So if you want pintucks in both directions and/or on the bias, try some out before making a final design.

● REMEMBER – pintucking is essentially 'fine' work, and if you stray too far from this, you will either make a horrid mess or stray into Tucks and Pleats.

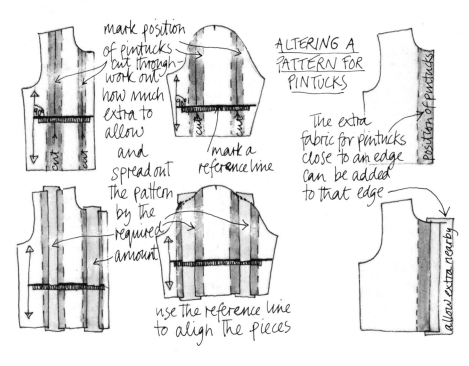

mark position of pintucks but through – work out how much extra to allow and spread out the pattern by the required amount

mark a reference line

use the reference line to align the pieces

ALTERING A PATTERN FOR PINTUCKS

The extra fabric for pintucks close to an edge can be added to that edge

position of pintucks

allow extra nearby

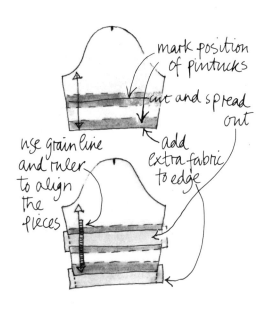

mark position of pintucks

cut and spread out

add extra fabric to edge

use grain line and ruler to align the pieces

This fake Victorian blouse worn by Rita Hayworth must have been one among hundreds made for historical films. They never look quite right, but the pintucked sleeves, yoke and neckband are not far wrong.

'Après la Danse'– separate panels pintucked and attached by the top edge to the skirt.

Left: Pintucks used on heavy coating accentuate the shoulders and decorate the sleeves of this 40s coat.

Choose a loose fitting jacket pattern with shoulder darts, set in sleeves and a straight, attached collar, plus a straight skirt pattern with darts, or tucks, at the waist (or if you can find it, use a pattern incorporating an outward facing pleat on each side of the front). For this version the shoulder darts are replaced with pintucks which match at the shoulder seams, with those stitched on the back in the form of a 'V'. Pintucks replace some (or all) of the ease on the sleeve head and shape in, slightly, the wrists. The front waist is subtly shaped by pintucks running into the patch pockets which are decorated to match the 'V' on the back. A pintucked belt holds in the remaining fullness at the waist. The skirt is adapted to make pleats, one on each side of the front, and stitched down to just below hip level, with a group of pintucks running parallel to them (Figs 1 and 2).

Both the jacket and skirt can be lined or unlined, as they are made up according to the instructions given with the pattern once the pintucks have been completed.

Variations

As you will see from Fig. 2, it is possible to make all the alterations shown or

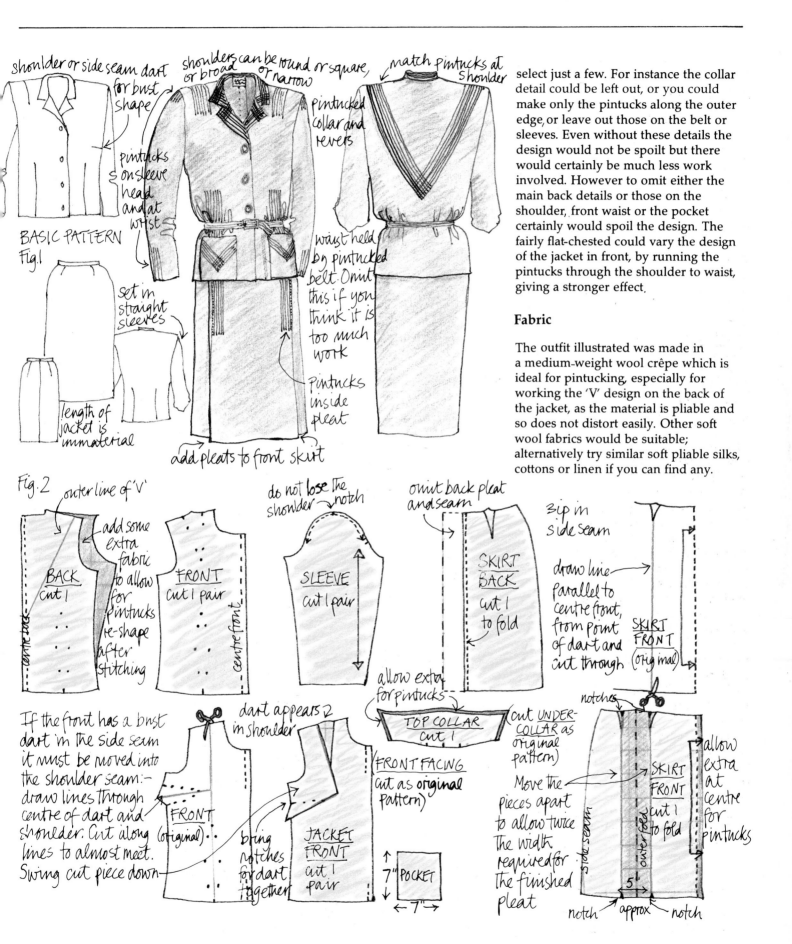

shoulder or side seam dart for bust shape

shoulders can be round or square, or broad or narrow

match pintucks at shoulder

pintucked collar and revers

pintucks on sleeve head and at wrist

BASIC PATTERN Fig. 1

set in straight sleeves

length of jacket is immaterial

waist held by pintucked belt. Omit this if you think it is too much work

Pintucks inside pleat

add pleats to front skirt

select just a few. For instance the collar detail could be left out, or you could make only the pintucks along the outer edge, or leave out those on the belt or sleeves. Even without these details the design would not be spoilt but there would certainly be much less work involved. However to omit either the main back details or those on the shoulder, front waist or the pocket certainly would spoil the design. The fairly flat-chested could vary the design of the jacket in front, by running the pintucks through the shoulder to waist, giving a stronger effect.

Fabric

The outfit illustrated was made in a medium-weight wool crêpe which is ideal for pintucking, especially for working the 'V' design on the back of the jacket, as the material is pliable and so does not distort easily. Other soft wool fabrics would be suitable; alternatively try similar soft pliable silks, cottons or linen if you can find any.

Fig. 2   outer line of 'V'

add some extra fabric to allow for pintucks re-shape after stitching

BACK cut 1

FRONT cut 1 pair

centre front

do not lose the shoulder notch

SLEEVE cut 1 pair

omit back pleat and seam

SKIRT BACK cut 1 to fold

zip in side seam

draw line parallel to centre front, from point of dart and cut through

SKIRT FRONT (original)

If the front has a bust dart in the side seam it must be moved into the shoulder seam:- draw lines through centre of dart and shoulder. Cut along lines to almost meet. Swing cut piece down

dart appears in shoulder

FRONT (original)

bring notches for dart together

JACKET FRONT cut 1 pair

allow extra for pintucks

TOP COLLAR cut 1

(cut UNDER-COLLAR as original pattern)

FRONT FACING (cut as original pattern)

7" POCKET

← 7" →

notches

Move the pieces apart to allow twice the width required for the finished pleat

side seam

outer edge

SKIRT FRONT cut 1 to fold

allow extra at centre for pintucks

notch   approx   notch

5"

Remember though that a fabric with a noticeably different warp and weft would probably not work too well for the 'V' motif shown here. Experiment first with the fabrics you like, sewing pintucks on the straight and bias before making the final choice.

Cutting out

As far as possible, follow the original fabric layout, as given in the pattern. The jacket will take very little extra fabric; the skirt will take quite a lot more, unless it has pleats already.
If you intend to line the jacket and skirt, cut out using the original pattern pieces.

For the jacket:
1 pair of fronts
1 pair of front facings, plus interlinings
1 back
1 pair sleeves
1 top collar, plus interlining
1 undercollar
1 pair of pockets
1 belt (for measurements, see under 'belt')

For the skirt:
1 front
1 back
1 waistband, plus interlining

Making up

Sleeves Make a group of pintucks on the sleevehead, each about 2 in. long (Fig. 3).
Note: if the sleevehead does not have any, or very little ease, it would be best to forget this detail.

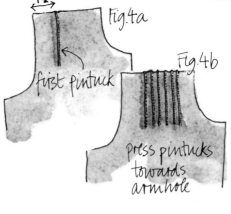

Fig.4a first pintuck

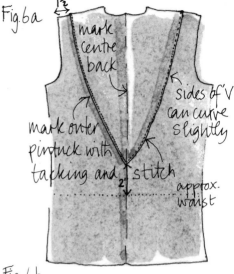

Fig.4b press pintucks towards armhole

Front Stitch the front shoulder pintucks. Start with the one nearest the shoulder which should be about 4in. long and running parallel to the dart line (Fig. 4a).
Work enough pintucks to take up the width of the dart at the shoulder seams. (If less are worked, the shoulder seam will be too long.) Therefore, if the shoulder dart is 1¼in. wide, eight or nine pintucks will be required to take up this amount (Fig. 4b). On the jacket shown, seven were stitched, ⅜in. apart. If your pattern has a very wide dart, make a narrow dart and take up the remainder with pintucks – as above (Fig. 4).

Back Mark the outer edge of the pintucked 'V' on to the back (Fig. 6a). Make sure that it matches the outer pintuck on the front. Use chalk and tack if necessary (see page 62). Stitch the first pintuck, working the point as described in the techniques on page 62 Work the remaining pintucks on one side, making the same number as on the front (so that

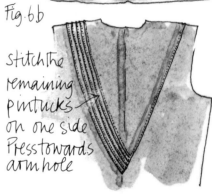

Fig.5 4" approx. line up pintucks approx 4" waist finish pintucks just above hem

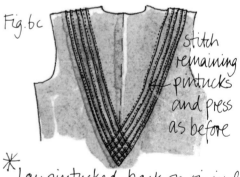

Fig 5a make pintucks on facings

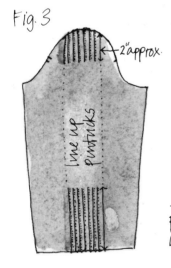

Fig.3 2" approx. line up pintucks

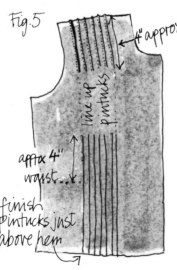

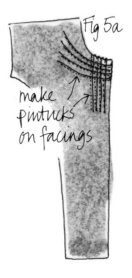

Fig.6a mark centre back mark outer pintuck with tacking and stitch sides of 'V' can curve slightly approx. waist

Fig.6b stitch the remaining pintucks on one side Press towards armhole

Fig.6c stitch remaining pintucks and press as before

✳ Lay pintucked back on original pattern and trim to fit.

the pintucked pattern will match when the shoulder seam is stitched), finishing off close up to the second side of the 'V', then press (Fig. 6b). Work the remaining pintucks on the second side, crossing the first, and finishing close to the first side of the 'V' (Fig. 6c). Press. Return to the jacket fronts and work the same number of pintucks at the waist as at the shoulder and in line with them (Fig. 5). Make pintucks on facings as shown in Fig. 5a.

Pockets Stitch the pintucks using the same method as given for the back (Fig. 7).

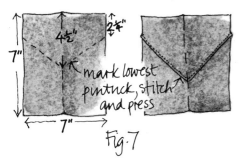

mark lowest pintuck, stitch and press

7"

7"

4½"

2¼"

Fig. 7

Stitch three more pintucks, press

Stitch the second group and press

Collar Mark the stitching line the width of the seam allowance from the outer edge (Fig. 8a). Stitch the pintucks across the ends and parallel to them, ⅜in. apart and the same distance inside the stitching line. Press firmly so that the pintucks turn towards the ends (Fig. 8b). Stitch pintucks along the length of the collar in the same way. Press so that the pintucks turn towards the free edge (Fig. 8c).

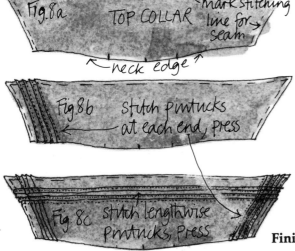

free edge

Fig.8a TOP COLLAR mark stitching line for seam

neck edge

Fig.8b stitch pintucks at each end, press

Fig.8c stitch lengthwise pintucks, press

Belt Cut a belt 4in. wide by your waist measurement, plus allowances for overlap etc. Press in half lengthways,

wrong sides together. Open out and work the first pintuck ⅜in. from the foldline and parallel to it, then work ork three more (Fig. 9a). Fold in half lengthways, this time right sides together and stitch with a ⅜in. seam allowance. Turn right side out and finish in the usual way (Fig. 9b).

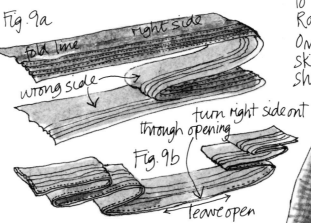

Fig. 9a

fold line right side

wrong side

turn right side ont through opening

Fig. 9b

leave open

Skirt front Press the pleats into position on the front, facing out towards the side seams (Fig. 10). Stitch the pintucks ⅜in. inside and parallel to the creased line, down as far as the pleat will be stitched. Press. Re-press the pleat into position and pin, then stitch the pleat down close to the pressed edge. Press.

Fig. 10 inner folds

pintucks

Stitch pleat in place to lower end of pintucks

outer folds

Finishing the jacket and skirt

Make up both as given in the original instructions, apart from omitting the darts on the jacket front and the ease on the sleevehead.

Variations:-

Button up to neck and stitch pintucks right through from shoulder to hem. Raise pockets. Omit pleats on skirt but make short pintucks in place of darts

Omit collar; pintuck neck and front edge; continue on skirt making concealed openings

Shape waist, with darts, to give close-fitting finish

peplum

Matching 'v' on skirt back above centre back pleat.

Appliqué

Appliqué, despite being the easiest of the ten techniques in this book,
is potentially the most decorative as it is unhampered by technical limitations.
Perhaps it is best thought of as a medium which, like paint,
can be used to make pictures and designs unlimited by colour, texture or shape,
and as simple or complicated as the dressmaker's imagination demands.
Almost anything made from fabric can be appliquéd –
a baby's romper suit with a rabbit – a ballgown with a garland of flowers –
a horse's blanket with initials – a cushion with a posy.
Nor does it need an artist to design it, as ideas can be cribbed from here,
there and everywhere, although artists such as the pre-Raphaelites
and sundry bohemians have espoused appliqué, decorating clothes
and household artefacts with beautiful, if occasionally eccentric, results.

◀ A detail from a curtain made by Sue Bodgenor.
The complete design shows three flowerheads surrounded by a border.
Some of the fabrics have been specially over-dyed.

This technique is really just a grand version of patching, which instead of covering up wears and tears, is used entirely for decoration. It is perhaps best used to decorate simple clothes with simple but bold motifs – label a shirt with initials on a pocket or transform a T-shirt with an emblem. Another attribute of appliqué is that it is cheap; it is not usually necessary to buy special fabric, especially if you already keep old clothes and off-cuts from dressmaking – though if you do decide to buy new, the tiny amounts needed for appliqué will not add much expense anyway.

● NOTE – that this chapter concentrates on machine-made appliqué. Handworked appliqué is really outside the realms of dressmaking.

simplicity is effective!

pocket decorations

Stitching on a patch pocket is a type of appliqué, so most dressmakers will already know the basic principles:

For a single motif draw the shape on paper and cut it out, use this as a pattern to cut the fabric from.
Lay in position on the piece to be appliquéd and pin. Then, using a small close zigzag, stitch all round the edges.

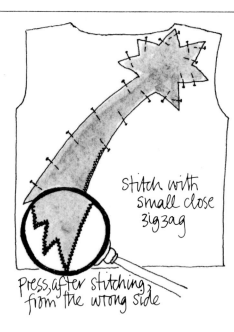

Stitch with small close zigzag

Press, after stitching, from the wrong side

Overlapping pieces. This can be done in various ways:
1 The pieces can be cut out as though they are complete and then either stitched on singly to build up the design piece by piece or all pinned on at the same time and stitched round, ignoring the concealed edges.

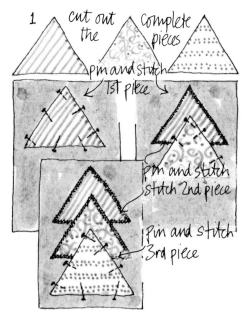

cut out the complete pieces

pin and stitch 1st piece

pin and stitch stitch 2nd piece

pin and stitch 3rd piece

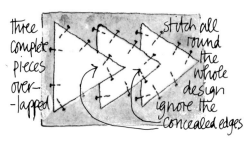

three complete pieces over-lapped

stitch all round the whole design ignore the concealed edges

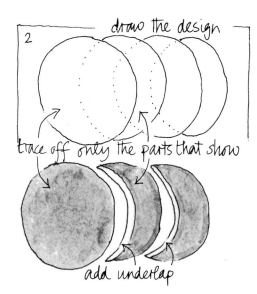

draw the design

trace off only the parts that show

add underlap

2 The pieces can have a small underlap added to the part which shows (instead of completing the piece). Pin on all the pieces and then stitch round.
3 The pieces can be cut to the shape which actually shows and each piece stitched separately round all its edges.

cut away the parts that do not show

pin and stitch all round 1st piece

pin and stitch all round 2nd and 3d pieces this method is useful with thick or stiff fabrics

● AVOID – stretching either the ground fabric or the appliqué pieces. Stitch a sample – if it tends to stretch, press the forefinger up against the back of the sewing foot. Experiment with the pressure until the result is quite flat, neither stretched nor compressed.

*Taken from a colour print, dated 1862. These
'Fashions of Paris' promote a ballgown, with blue
appliqué around the hem. The figure at the back is
more soberly clad in purple and black.*

Above: Another French print, possibly the design for a fancy dress costume. The literal translation of Pervenche Dessechée is 'withered Periwinkle'! Top left: Modern fancy dress from Montana. Space-age in effect, there are unicorns and an armour-like yoke appliquéd onto the bodice, plus wide belt and decorated hem. The wing-style whisk on the arm completes the fantasy look. Left: Dressing up clothes from the 70s. The author made this kaftan for herself; now it's been remade into a jacket and skirt.

Seam allowances are not necessary unless the fabric is loosely woven or tends to fray, or if a straight stitch is going to be used. If this is the case, the allowances must be added after tracing off the design and before cutting out. They should be kept as narrow as possible: ¼in. is usually ample. Cut out and press the seam allowances to the wrong side; lay the pieces in position as before and machine using a straight or zigzag stitch. (Of course the seam allowances need not be pressed to the wrong side if they are going to be overlapped by another piece.)

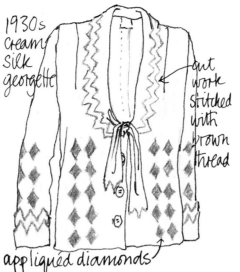

1930s creamy silk georgette

cut work stitched with brown thread

appliqued diamonds

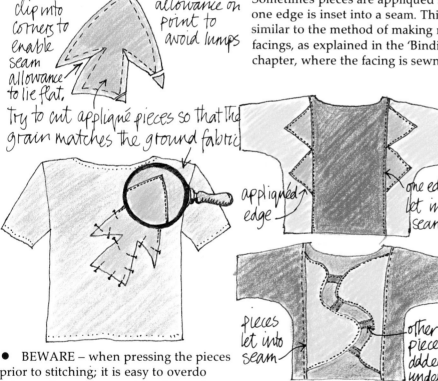

clip into corners to enable seam allowance to lie flat.

cut back allowance on point to avoid lumps

Try to cut appliqué pieces so that the grain matches the ground fabric

appliquéd edge

one edge let into seam

pieces let into seam

other pieces added underneath

'reverse' facings appliquéd in place on inner edge

- BEWARE – when pressing the pieces prior to stitching; it is easy to overdo this, causing an impression of the edges to show on the right side. The stitching will hold the edge flat so it is not necessary to press too heavily.

- ADD – decoration to appliqué. The pieces can be embroidered by hand or machine, either before or after they are stitched down. Also the stitching can be extended past the edges of the piece, or beads and sequins added before or after the pieces are stitched in place.

Inset appliqué

Sometimes pieces are appliquéd so that one edge is inset into a seam. This is similar to the method of making reverse facings, as explained in the 'Bindings' chapter, where the facing is sewn onto the wrong side, brought over to the right side and the edge stitched down. These facings can be cut in quite complicated shapes but would probably need to have seam allowances added and be laid down with a straight stitch, though this does depend on current styles and the fabric and design being used.

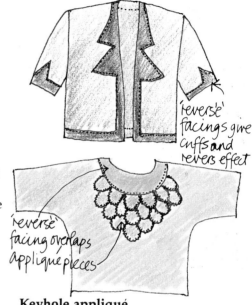

'reverse' facings give cuffs and revers effect

'reverse' facing overlaps appliqué pieces

Keyhole appliqué

Net, lace and other transparent fabrics are often used for this, particularly to decorate underwear, blouses and evening clothes. In the past, flesh coloured satin or crêpe was often inset underneath the net for reasons of modesty; this is not required nowadays, but who knows what fashion will do next?

pin shaped piece onto wrong side and zigzag edges

trim main fabric away (from right side) inside line of stitching

77

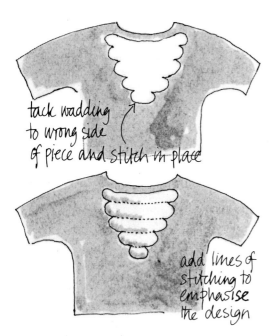

tack wadding to wrong side of piece and stitch in place

add lines of stitching to emphasise the design

Quilted appliqué

Although this is covered in many specialist books it is worth mentioning here as occasionally it becomes a fashionable dressmaking technique. It certainly adds another decorative facet. Individual motifs can be appliquéd and then stuffed with wadding, through a hole, from the back of the main fabric, or the wadding can be tacked to the appliqué pieces and stitched down as one piece. In either case, hand or machine stitching can be added as further decoration. Conversely flat pieces of appliqué can be sewn onto a piece of fabric that will subsequently be completely quilted.

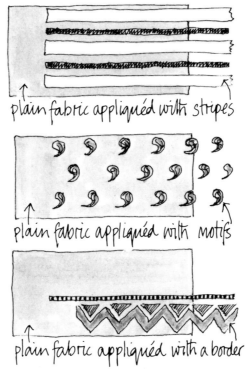

collar and cuffs cut in colour to match print

jacket appliquéd with motif cut from trouser fabric

● AVOID – using stiff fabrics for quilting. Soft, supple or slightly stretchy materials such as wool or cotton jersey, crêpes, soft wools and cottons and the softer satins are most suitable because they will take to the three dimensional shape better.

Fabric

In the right place, any fabric can be decorated with appliqué or used to appliqué another. This is not to say that georgette should be decorated with canvas sailcloth! But georgette can be appliquéd with the selfsame fabric or something equally lightweight to make blouses and nightdresses – and canvas can be appliquéd onto canvas for simply decorated jackets, coats and bags. Woven or knitted, thick or thin, soft or stiff, opaque or transparent, smooth or textured, glossy or dull, plain or patterned – all can be part of the appliqué maker's fabric palette. Thick

plain fabric appliquéd with stripes

plain fabric appliquéd with motifs

plain fabric appliquéd with a border

materials can be appliquéd with thinner ones of the same or a different colour and texture, or try net or velvet appliquéd with silk or cotton – or vice versa. And what about tweed with tweed, exploiting the subtly changing colours and different weaves?

Kimono of plain fabric appliquéd with borders and motifs

● BE WARNED – thin fabrics tend not to hang well when appliquéd with thicker or stiffer fabrics – but there are always exceptions waiting to be explored for some special purpose, perhaps to hold out a skirt or stiffen a collar.

● REMEMBER – to consider how the fabric will hang after the appliqué pieces have been sewn on. To facilitate this, match the grain on both fabrics, especially if the pieces are large.

Stitches

Straight stitches can always be used but I almost always use zigzag, as I prefer to treat the stitching as part of the design. However, different pieces of work require different solutions. All sizes and variations of zigzag can be used, but the stitch should always suit the fabric – a wide open zigzag, though perfectly satisfactory on some fabrics, might not hold the pieces neatly on a loose weave with a tendency to fray.

● EXPERIMENT – with fabrics that *do* fray, in case something interesting happens.

1981
net
appliqued
with cotton
leaves

Emmanuelle Kahn.

- REMEMBER – closely woven fabrics can be stitched down with zigzag without a seam allowance – just stitch over the raw edge and then trim off the whiskers! If extra colour or emphasis is needed, a thicker thread can be couched down under the zigzag stitching.

- AVOID – making the stitches so close that they make the fabric stiff – unless that is, you are planning to use this stiffened effect in some way, to emphasise the puffiness of a sleeve or the shape of a pocket for instance.

Thread

This should be considered right from the beginning as it can become a feature of the design. The colour can match or contrast with either the ground fabric or the appliqué pieces, or different types and colours of threads can be used within one piece of work.

When zigzag stitches are going to be used, the thread is obviously more important than for straight stitching, and

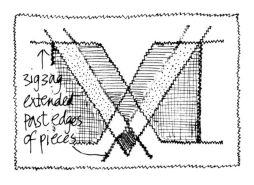

zigzag extended past edges of pieces

in either case machine embroidery threads are sometimes used to give a glossy finish. Generally speaking, the finest machine thread is quite strong enough used with zigzag, especially if the stitches are worked close together. For straight stitches, particularly on thicker fabrics, thin thread will probably not wear well enough and a thicker one will be more satisfactory. Occasionally heavier thread can be used deliberately to emphasise or stiffen the edges, as has already been mentioned.

Pressing

If there is a seam allowance try to press from the wrong side to avoid impressions showing through on the right side – both when pressing edges to the wrong side and after stitching pieces on. Do not overdo it; the stitching will hold the edges flat so it is not necessary to press heavily. Where there is no seam allowance the work can be pressed from either side depending on the fabric used. Thoroughly dampening the fabric with a laundry spray will help to shrink out wrinkles after the pieces are stitched in place.

Children and appliqué

Children enjoy decorating clothes, so as soon as they can handle scissors let them start appliqué.

Cut out a simple waistcoat from felt in one piece, then let the child work out its own ideas, cutting directly into scraps of felt or fabric. Older children might prefer to work out a design first on paper while younger ones could be given ready-cut-out shapes to arrange.

Glue and staples are popular for fixing the pieces in place, but most children can manage a sewing machine, if given the opportunity, from about the age of seven or eight.

When I showed children of this age how to make these waistcoats they became a veritable school uniform, decorated with unlikely designs featuring anything from dinosaurs and skulls to stars and space rockets, incorporating besides beads, buttons and sequins, odd pieces of junk such as tap washers, often all held together with large numbers of staples!

shape for waistcoat pattern

simple shapes can make interesting designs

staples

beads

striped bias cut bindings

buttons

mixtures of embroidery and coloured felt

pinked strips stitched round edges

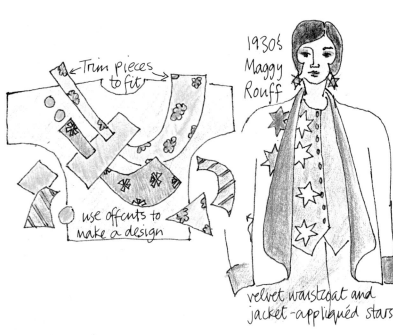

← Trim pieces to fit →

use offcuts to make a design

1930s Maggy Rouff

velvet waistcoat and jacket-appliquéd stars

Poncho appliqué and

Designing for appliqué

As any two-dimensional idea can be used for appliqué, it is only necessary to find a way of translating it into cloth. Generally simple designs are more effective than complex ones, although a more intricate design made by a really neat-fingered sewer can look beautiful. However, unless you have a great deal of patience and time, it is better to stick to the former which is anyway probably more in tune with the times.

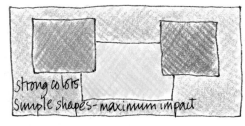

strong colors
Simple shapes – maximum impact

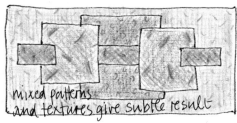

mixed patterns and textures give subtle result

Look for inspiration in paintings and photographs, postcards and flowers, books on design, letters, numbers, anywhere and everywhere. Artists such as Matisse, Miro and Delaunay are good for strong images.

Collect scraps of fabrics in all colours, both plain and patterned, and of different textures and degrees of transparency. Use these like paints to colour in a design, shuffling the scraps around until you are happy with the result. Use opaque fabrics for solid colours whilst sheer colours can be used to build up layers of colour in a similar way to a painter using washes of water colour.

● EXPERIMENT – with subtle changes of texture. A shiny fabric appliquéd with various rough or dull pieces, all in the same colour, might be interesting.

Texture can be added by fraying, painting, embroidering (by hand or machine) or brushing with a wire brush to make the surface rough or to raise a pile. Threads can be drawn to change the character of a fabric or unusual fabrics such as straw cloth and plastics introduced.

● REMEMBER – a single idea used well will have more impact than several, however well done. Be judicious – select the best, discard the rest.

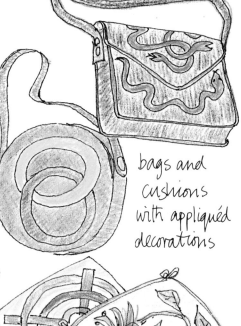

bags and cushions with appliquéd decorations

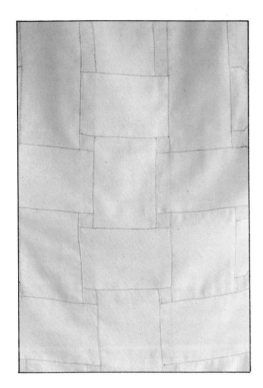

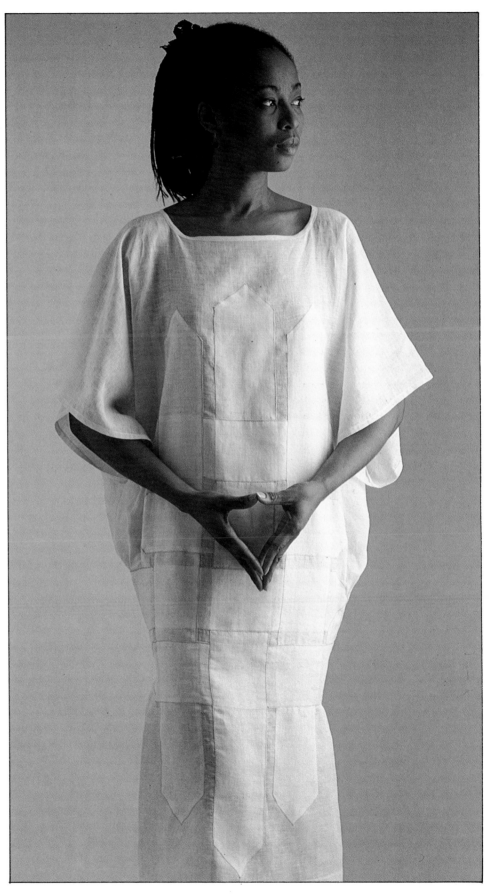

As the main part of the appliqué can be stitched in place before the seams are sewn up this dress is really simple to make. The motif was designed to use appliqué both as decoration and as part of the structure of the garment. So the hip bands hold in the tucks at the hips and the remaining bands, apart from being decorative, help to make the slightly transparent fabric more opaque and thus easier to wear. Similar motifs could be applied to all sorts of things, such as the back of a cloak, the front of a smock, curtains, cushions or loose covers.

The pattern

The sample was made from a one-piece pattern, but any simple dress without a waist and loose rather than close fitting could be decorated in a similar way. (Figs 1, 2 and 3.)

Note: Check that your pattern is large enough around the hips to allow for the tucks, or make the tucks narrower.

The motif

There are four horizontal and three vertical bands. The two lower horizontal bands form a hip band and continue, each in one piece, onto the back, holding

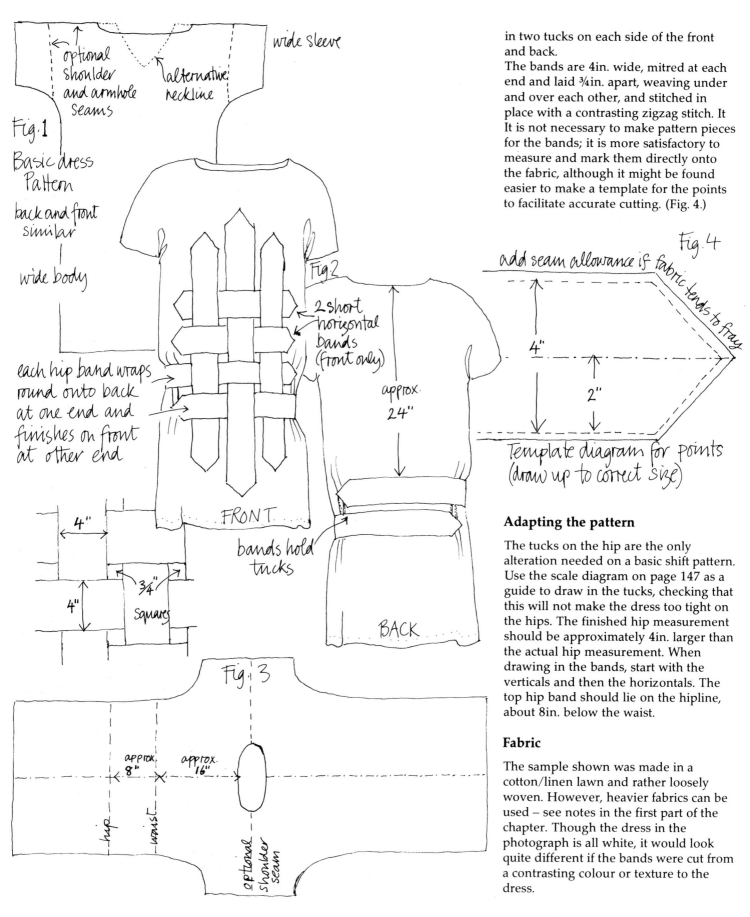

Fig.1

Basic dress Pattern

back and front similar

wide body

optional shoulder and armhole seams

alternative neckline

wide sleeve

each hip band wraps round onto back at one end and finishes on front at other end

Fig.2

2 short horizontal bands (front only)

approx. 24"

FRONT

bands hold tucks

BACK

4"

4"

3/4" Squares

Fig.3

approx. 8"

approx. 16"

hip

waist

optional shoulder seam

in two tucks on each side of the front and back.

The bands are 4in. wide, mitred at each end and laid ¾in. apart, weaving under and over each other, and stitched in place with a contrasting zigzag stitch. It It is not necessary to make pattern pieces for the bands; it is more satisfactory to measure and mark them directly onto the fabric, although it might be found easier to make a template for the points to facilitate accurate cutting. (Fig. 4.)

Fig.4

add seam allowance if fabric tends to fray

4"

2"

Template diagram for points (draw up to correct size)

Adapting the pattern

The tucks on the hip are the only alteration needed on a basic shift pattern. Use the scale diagram on page 147 as a guide to draw in the tucks, checking that this will not make the dress too tight on the hips. The finished hip measurement should be approximately 4in. larger than the actual hip measurement. When drawing in the bands, start with the verticals and then the horizontals. The top hip band should lie on the hipline, about 8in. below the waist.

Fabric

The sample shown was made in a cotton/linen lawn and rather loosely woven. However, heavier fabrics can be used – see notes in the first part of the chapter. Though the dress in the photograph is all white, it would look quite different if the bands were cut from a contrasting colour or texture to the dress.

If the fabric has a very open weave or tends to fray easily, add seam allowances to the bands and use an open zigzag, otherwise use a close zigzag over the cut edges; it is worth experimenting with this as, given a little practise, it is surprising how many fabrics can be perfectly finished in this way.

Thread

The zigzag stitch used on the sample was an ordinary machine embroidery thread in blue, thus accenting the motif.

Cutting out

1 Back
1 Front (or 1 back and front together)
3 Vertical bands
4 Horizontal bands

Making up

Neck edge Finish this first to avoid fraying or stretching with a narrow bias strip cut from the same fabric.

Tucks Mark, press, pin and stitch the tucks, using the scale diagram on page 147 as a guide.

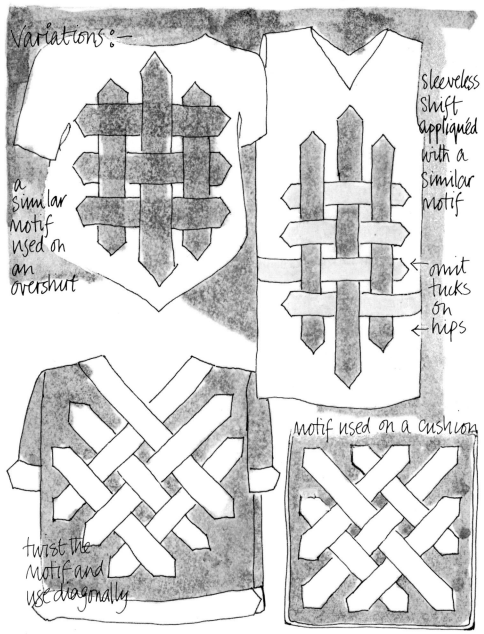

Variations:—

a similar motif used on an overshirt

sleeveless shift appliquéd with a similar motif

← omit tucks on ← hips

twist the motif and use diagonally

motif used on a cushion

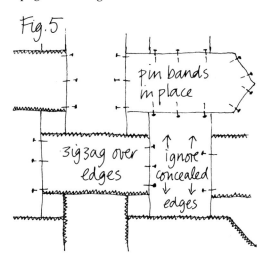

Fig. 5

pin bands in place

zigzag over edges

ignore concealed edges

Bands Fold and press the centre front and back to make a crease to help with placing the bands. Do this accurately. Then press the seam allowances on the bands, if any, to the wrong side.
Lay the front of the pattern out flat, right side up. Lay the front of the dress out beside it, also right side up.

Measuring off from the pattern, mark the position of the ends of the vertical bands. Pin them in position. Do the same for the horizontal bands, weaving them in and out according to Fig. 2.
Check that everything *looks* right; this is more important than being right!
Stitch the bands in place using an open zigzag if there is a seam allowance, a close zigzag if not. Sew the zigzag stitching exactly on the edge on the band. (Fig. 5.)

Note: Do not zigzag across the concealed edges of the bands. The two hip hands should be left free at the ends where they continue across the side seams at this stage.

Front and back If the fabric is at all transparent, make the side, underarm and shoulder seams (if included) using French seams. Otherwise use ordinary seams. Press.
Pin the hip bands in position around the back, again measuring from the pattern, and stitch with zigzag to match the front.

Finishing off Finish the sleeve ends and hem to match the neck.
From the wrong side, catch down the unstitched, concealed edges of the bands by hand, making sure the stitches do not show on the right side.

Bands and Bindings

The origin of bindings lay in the necessity to finish cut edges neatly –
easy enough on fine fabrics, not so easy on heavy ones such as those used for coats.
So a method of wrapping thinner fabrics around the cut edge evolved,
thus producing a 'binding'.
Gradually, special folded braids were developed to supplement the original strips,
which became more and more decorative, culminating in the nineteenth century with a
bonanza of bands and bindings trimming fabrics of all weights.
Probably the best known practitioner of this technique was Chanel,
whose beautiful suits, based on simple shapes, were invariably trimmed with bindings.
The design of her clothes used alongside the notes given in this chapter
should be enough to inspire anyone to try their hand with bindings.

◀ *A memorial pouch by Patricia Saunders.*
Decorated with small bands, bound edges, embroidery and faggoting, with ribbon detail.
Many of the fabrics have been hand-dyed to achieve the required muted effect.

Most people associate bindings entirely with cards of bias binding. This is sad because, once the basic technique has been learnt, bindings open up an easy way to use heavier fabrics, which are often considered difficult to handle. There are two main categories of bindings:

● Braid or tape, woven especially for bindings, ready-folded with 'finished' (that is not raw, or cut) edges.

● Strips cut from fabric, generally on the bias and folded in half. These of course have the disadvantage of raw edges and take time to cut and press, but they provide far more freedom in choice of colour and fabric.

Fabrics for bands and bindings

These should usually be closely woven, thin and strong. However, as almost any fabric can be bound, a wide variety of fabrics can be used for the bands and bindings.

Avoid anything stiff and remember that a fabric used satisfactorily to bind a wool coat may not be equally satisfactory for binding a linen skirt.

Consider whether the bindings and bands will be curved or straight. If curved, they must be cut on the cross and a suitably pliable fabric chosen; whereas for straight bands, almost any fabric of the right weight can be used, whether using the straight or the bias grain.

● EXPERIMENT – with fabrics of different weight, texture and weave. Try out short pieces of fabric to see what effect the binding has in relation to the main fabric – how it hangs – how bulky – how stiff.

Never use stretchy fabrics for binding except with an industrial stretch stitch overlocker if you happen to have access to one. But stretchy fabrics can be bound; indeed this is often the best way to deal with jersey fabrics as the binding can be used not just decoratively, but to stop it stretching.

Poplin, lawn and other cotton fabrics of a similar weight are widely used for bindings. Try also lightweight needle-cord or velveteen, Viyella or other wool/cotton mixtures, lightweight silks and woollens.

● REMEMBER – a bound edge will be five layers thick which must make some extra bulk. Will the particular fabric you have in mind look nice or simply lumpy?

The stitching

Usually an ordinary straight machine stitch is best, not so small that it stiffens the seam, nor so large that it does not hold the binding properly. Zigzag looks decorative and can also be extra strong.

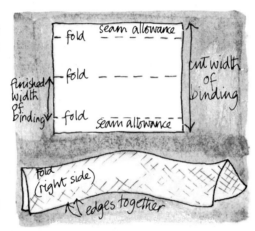

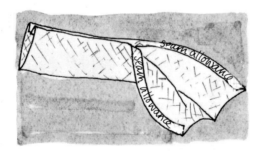

Cutting a binding

The binding consists of four parts: the part that will show as the binding on the right side when finished, a similar part which will show on the wrong side, and two seam allowances which will be hidden.

Decide on the finished width, double it, and add twice the seam allowance required. Often the seam allowance is the same as the finished width of the binding, but sometimes it is less.

Read the notes on bias cutting in 'Piping' and then cut strips to the required width. Fold the strip in half and press with wrong sides together.

Stitching on cut bindings

Open out the binding and lay the right side on the wrong side of the edge to be bound, so that when it is stitched and pressed, the folded edge comes tight up against the cut edge (i.e. the binding does not project past the cut edge).

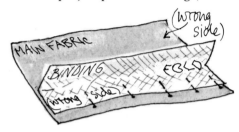

Pin in place. Stitch exactly the allowed amount from the edge of the binding.

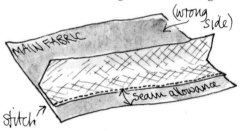

Press the binding so that it lies over the seam allowance.

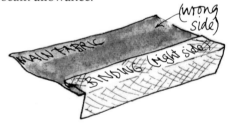

Next press the seam allowance on the free edge of the bias strip onto the wrong side. Bring this edge down to lie along the stitching line and pin in place.

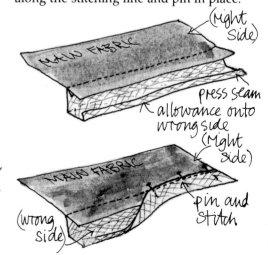

Top: Amateur bands on sunsuit. A competitor at a
seaside fashion contest smiles winningly at the
judges! Above: A Breton in national costume; the
jacket features pinked bands and bindings. Right:
Marlene Dietrich in a classic 1940s suit with
bound edges.

It should lie absolutely flat if the seam allowances have been observed accurately. Topstitch very close to the edge of the binding. This is the simplest, probably the neatest, and certainly the most widely used method of applying a binding. It can be used for all cut bindings, including 'bought' or 'readymade' bias binding. If the row of topstitching is not wanted, reverse the method of sewing on the binding: start instead by laying the binding on the right side of the edge to be bound so that the second free edge ends up pinned on the wrong side. The pinned edge can then be slipstitched into place by hand. However, this method is practically never used nowadays on ready-made clothes, even the most expensive. It is slow and unless the tiniest of stitches are used, tends to give a 'homemade' look.

A better method is to press a smaller seam allowance on the free edge so that it will overlap the stitching line slightly. Pin it in place. Turn to the right side and stitch on the main fabric, very close to the binding. This is another method used widely on ready-made clothing giving a flat, neat finish.

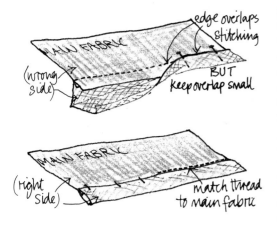

- NOTE – An edge that is going to be bound needs no seam allowance as nothing is lost when the binding is

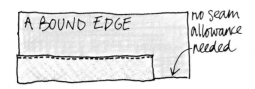

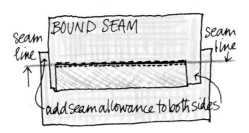

wrapped over the edge. However, on a bound lapped seam, seam allowances must be allowed for.

- PLAN AHEAD – when designing a garment. Work out in advance whether seam allowances will be needed, remembering that this may vary on one garment. Choose a method that will look neat on the right and wrong sides if both sides of the garment are to show.

Ready-made bindings

These are generally available from haberdashers as mentioned before, they are ready-folded and as the edges are finished and do not need neatening, very easy to use.

Usually made from cotton, wool or rayon in various widths, they can be flat and thin, or thick and bulky and variously textured – smooth or rough, glossy or dull.

Colour is the main problem, as they are usually found only in the most basic of colours – black, white and grey, with the occasional bright red and royal blue. To overcome this limitation, I have successfully dyed several different types in colours to contrast with the rest of a garment. If you decide to do this, do find out what the binding is made of at the time of buying as dyes take to different fibres in different ways. Remember also to consider the comparative weight and bulk of the binding and the fabric to be bound. Obviously no-one would use a thick wool, or probably any wool binding on a lightweight cotton fabric, but this principle extends with increasing degrees of subtlety to the choice of binding for any fabric. I keep a stock of ready-made bindings, especially in unusual colours, plus various types of white ones ready to dye. It is surprising how often they come in useful, even if it is only to make little purses, dolls' clothes, or finish the edges of a cushion.

- BEWARE – of ready-made bias bindings. They are often made from poor quality cotton, and the dyes are not necessarily fast. If it is worth binding something, it is worth cutting it yourself from a better fabric that you know will wash and wear well.

Stitching on ready-made bindings

Binding that is folded exactly in half is usually opened out and stitched twice, first on the wrong side, and then after being refolded, stitched on the right side.

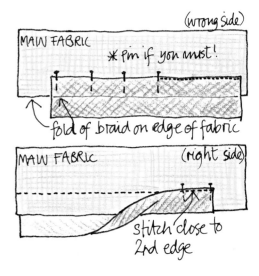

Some bindings are folded so that one side is slightly wider than the other; these are the easiest of all to apply. Simply lap the binding over the edge to be bound, with the wider side on the wrong side, and then stitch close to the edge from the right side.

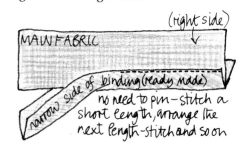

If you are a confident machinist, however, you can also sew the evenly folded binding on in this way – but it might be a good idea to practise first.

● REMEMBER – wrap the binding tightly over the cut edge so that the fold of the binding is right on the cut edge. If the binding is stitched too near the edge, it is less firm, and the binding could pull away due to fraying.

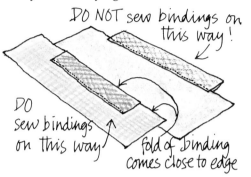

DO NOT sew bindings on this way!

DO sew bindings on this way

fold of binding comes close to edge

● NOTE – fabric bindings can be folded and pressed so that one side is wider, to enable it to be stitched on with one row of stitching (as above). But the extra time needed to press bindings so accurately might be longer than that taken to stitch twice. But for those who prefer pressing to machining, this has obvious advantages.

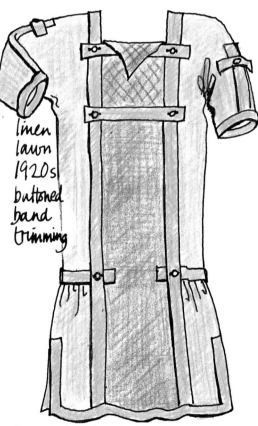

linen lawn 1920s buttoned band trimming

Two coats from the 1960s showing a dramatic use of bands on simple wraparound styles.

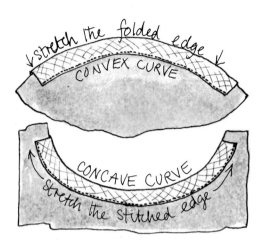

Binding curves

Because bindings are cut on the bias – or in the case of ready-made bindings, specially woven – they are pliable and readily take to curves. Usually, pulling the binding on the edge that is to go around the outside of the curve, stretches it enough to allow it to lie flat when stitched. The tighter the curve, the more the appropriate edge will need stretching.

On convex curves this is not much of a problem because the stitched free edges can be drawn up, thus increasing the curve. On concave curves this cannot be done, because the folded edge cannot be drawn up satisfactorily, so in this case curves should be kept fairly shallow.

● REMEMBER – a wide binding used on a curve will need more stretching than a narrow binding used on the same curve, because the difference between the two sides increases with the width.

There are various ways in which to draw up the free edges of the binding. For small amounts, hold the point of the scissors tight up against the back of the

presser foot, thus resisting the binding as it is stitched, causing it to draw up slightly (without forming gathers). Of course this must be done on both sides of the binding separately before it is stitched on.

There is also the opposite method; pushing the fabric under the presser foot from the front so that small tucks form, again using the point of the scissors and again on each side of the binding. A third method is to make tiny gathering stitches by hand or machine along the free edge of the binding and then draw it up in appropriate places. This is a bit fiddly, but if you like handwork, not difficult.

Note: on the whole it is best to start with a simple shallow curves; experience will allow progress to deeper more complex ones.

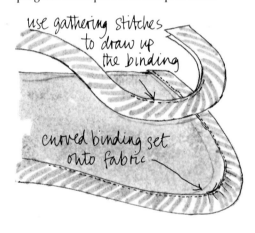

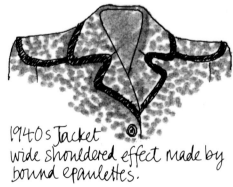

1940s Jacket wide shouldered effect made by bound epaulettes.

Binding corners is not as difficult as you might think.

Stitch along the first side, leaving the needle down, then lift the presser foot and turn the fabric ready to stitch the second side. Pull the binding round, folding the corners neatly so that small pleats form, to face one way on top and in the opposite direction underneath.

Pocket with binding mitred at the corners

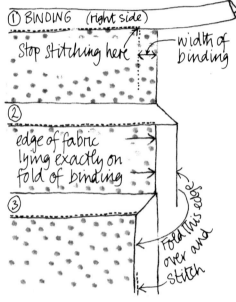

Lap it around the main fabric, drop the presser foot and stitch the second side. Alternatively the binding can be pinned, or pinned and tacked, and then stitched. The disadvantage to both these methods, lies in the tendency of all bindings to stretch when they are stitched, thus producing little wrinkles or pleats. To overcome this problem, stretch the binding slightly as you pin or tack. This must not be overdone, of course, or the binding will look too small and the fabric being bound may pucker and not lie flat. The amount by which to stretch the binding can only be learned by experience, so experiment until you have a feel for it.

● PRACTISE – sewing on binding without tacking, perhaps using a pin at the corners as you come to them. This obviously saves time, so do try it.

● A SHORT CUT – which can sometimes be used is to round off corners slightly, and then work them as for tight curves.

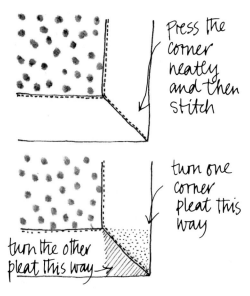

Press the corner neatly and then stitch

turn one corner pleat this way

turn the other pleat this way

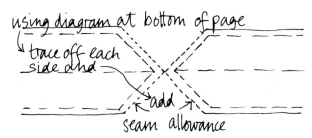

using diagram at bottom of page

trace off each side and

add

seam allowance

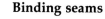

Stay stitch around the point

trim point

Mitring cut fabric bindings

If the bindings are narrow, follow the techniques given for the ready-made variety as described. Wider ones, however, are inclined to look messy done in this way, though sometimes the angled pleat formed at a corner can be stitched down flat by machine.

● DO – fold the pleats on each side of the binding to face in opposite directions to avoid bulky corners.

● EXPERIMENT – with accurately cut paper strips to understand how to fold a corner and so save fabric later on.

Joined mitres can be made by extending the method above. To stitch, lay the two pieces right sides together and machine around the point.

Other mitres are sometimes required which are not an angle of 45°. The easiest way to cope with these is to think of the mitre as an ordinary seam and mark the binding (or bands) on the pattern, stitch in the usual way.

● REMEMBER – be very accurate with seam allowances at all stages.

trace off binding

collar pattern

cut binding using pattern

mark line for binding and mitre

Binding seams

Besides binding the edges of a garment, one side of a seam can be bound; lap it over the other side and topstitch in place. This extends the design potential as the edges and seams can be co-ordinated. It also makes fitting and managing shaped seams easier, particularly on heavy fabrics or those which have a tendency to 'wriggle'. The binding is stitched onto one side of the seam, lapped over the second side and pinned whilst fitting the garment and subsequently topstitched from the right side. This makes it easy to see exactly what you are doing.

This method is also useful on seams that are tightly curved, such as armholes and sleeveheads, which can be difficult to put together accurately, especially if thick fabrics are involved.

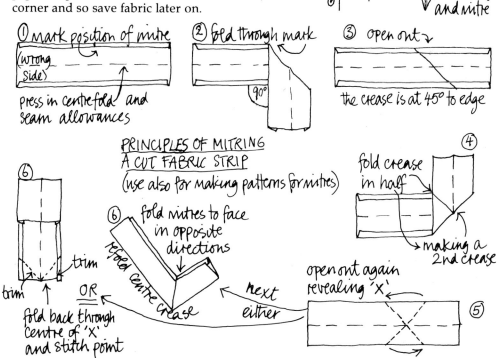

① *mark position of mitre* (wrong side) *press in centrefold and seam allowances*

② *fold through mark* 90°

③ *open out* *the crease is at 45° to edge*

④ *fold crease in half* *making a 2nd crease*

⑤ *open out again revealing 'x'*

next either

⑥ *fold mitres to face in opposite directions* *folded centre crease*

⑥ *fold back through centre of 'x' and stitch point*

OR

trim

PRINCIPLES OF MITRING A CUT FABRIC STRIP (use also for making patterns for mitres)

Late 1940s inspired by 'The New Look' –

close fitting waist, full skirt and bust emphasised by bound curved seams

Shocking pink taffeta with contrast binding, buttons and bows

Seams with bands

Seams can also have bands stitched over them, either to decorate, or to neaten, or both. Use readymade flat (i.e. not double) bindings, ribbon, tape or braid, or cut them from fabric on the straight or bias grain, depending on the seam. The seam can be sewn the wrong way out, so that the seam shows on the right side and then a band sewn down over the seam allowance, so making a neat 'inside' to the garment. Or the reverse, sew the seam the usual way round, again stitching the binding over the seam allowance, perhaps using a zigzag stitch. Either of these methods could be used for making reversible garments.

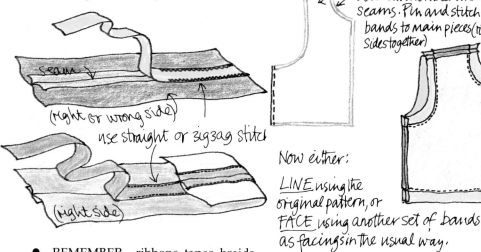

seam

(right or wrong side)

use straight or zigzag stitch

(right side)

- REMEMBER – ribbons, tapes, braids and bias-cut strips can be stitched onto garments to form patterns anywhere you like. Use contrasting or toning colours and work out a design on the paper pattern first.

Inset bands

These are usually shaped but occasionally straight bands set generally into the edge of a garment and then treated as though they are part of the garment, that is ignored, for lining or facing purposes. To make up, be very accurate with seam allowances or the pieces will not fit together properly. Set the bands on carefully and then press them thoroughly; the seam allowances can be pressed open or to either side, depending on the fabric and the effect required. The facing or lining – cut using the original pattern – can then be set on in the usual way, ignoring the band.

Making a pattern for inset bands mark lines for bands (or facings) on the pattern

BAND and/or FACING PATTERNS

trace off and add seam allowances

do the same

with the main pieces (i.e front and back) Join all shoulder and side seams. Pin and stitch bands to main pieces (right sides together)

Now either:

LINE using the original pattern, or FACE using another set of bands as facings in the usual way.

Reverse facings

Sometimes edges are bound using the same method as for facings, except that the binding or facing is first stitched onto the wrong side and the free edge topstitched in place on the right side, so making a decorative feature.

For reverse facings cut bands as above – BUT – cut main pieces from original pattern. Join shoulder and side seams. Lay right side of facing on wrong side of main piece, stitch. Trim corners, clip curves. Press facing to lie on right side of garment and press seam allowance on free edges onto wrong side.

(right side)

Pin inner edges in place and top stitch

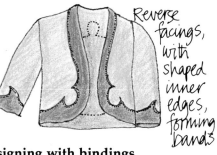

Reverse facings, with shaped inner edges, forming bands

Designing with bindings

It is important, as with all the techniques in this book, to remember the limitations as well as the advantages. Bindings can emphasise a design by outlining the edges and seams, or finish edges, or make seams easy to adjust and sew. However, they are difficult to manage on tight curves, especially if thick or stiff fabrics are being used. Nor should you use them to navigate too many curves and corners if you ever want to finish a garment, as they take a long time. The best advice is to use bindings boldly and simply, and as far as possible decorating and neatening in one operation.

1930s viscose crêpe

silky ribbon bands stitched on forming a geometric design

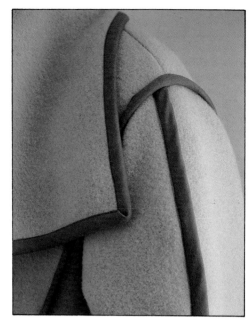

A warm, practical coat that helps to lift the gloom of a winter's day is a welcome addition to most wardrobes. This one is simpler to make than most coats, both because the double-faced brushed wool fabric needs no lining, and because the edges are bound, there are no facings and hems to make.

Fabric

Aim for the thickest, softest wool you can find; it must be double-faced, that is with both sides brushed or 'finished', as both will show.

For the binding, read the notes on 'fabrics' in the first part of the chapter, remembering that as the main fabric is very thick, it is important to use a thin binding, whether you are using a ready-made one or cutting your own.

Thread

Choose one to match the main fabric and one to match the binding.

Adapting the pattern

Start with a simple coat pattern which should be very loose fitting in the body, sleeves and armholes, with wide shoulders (Fig. 1a).

On the coat shown in Fig. 1b, the sleeve pattern has been cut through the centre and the seam curved to produce a separate front and back (Figs. 2a and b). (Alternatively, if you would prefer a straight sleeve, make the centre seam straight.) Alter the front as Fig. 3a, tracing off a side front panel and the main front, and a pocket bag if required (Fig. 3b).

Alter the back as shown, tracing off the yoke and the main back piece (Fig. 3a). Pin the pattern for the side front to the main back at the side seams so that the back and side fronts will be cut in one piece (i.e. no side seam) (Fig. 4).

Cutting out

1 pair fronts
1 main back (including side fronts)
1 back yoke
1 pair front sleeves
1 pair back sleeves
1 pair pocket bags – cut from thin fabric
Enough bias strips to bind the whole coat

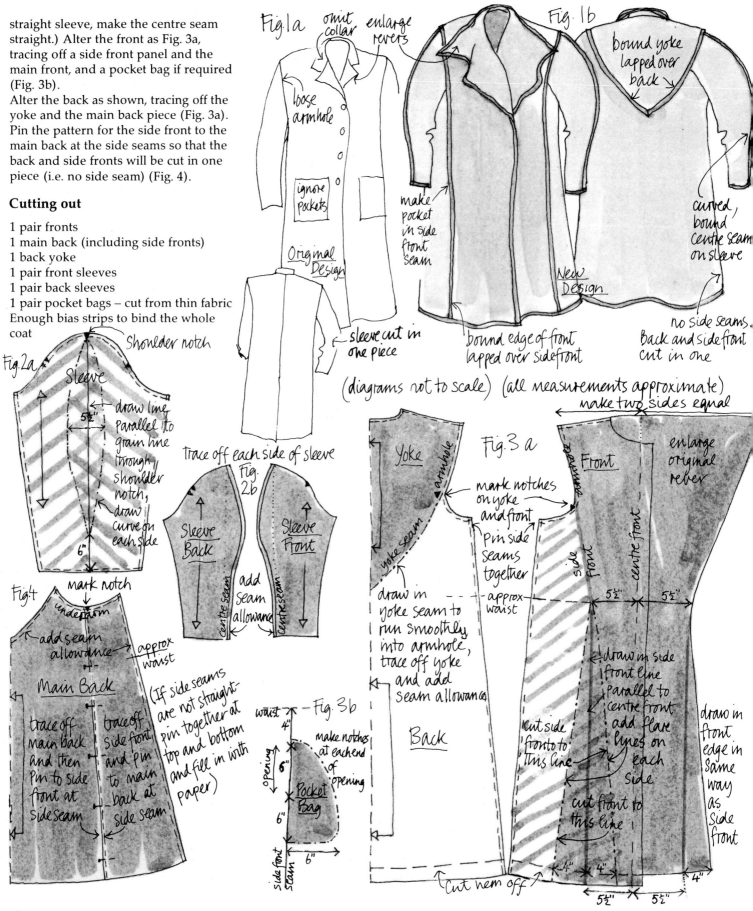

Fig. 1a omit collar enlarge revers
loose armhole
ignore pockets
Original Design
sleeve cut in one piece

Fig. 1b
bound yoke lapped over back
make pocket in side front seam
New Design
bound edge of front lapped over sidefront
curved, bound centre seam on sleeve
no side seams. Back and side front cut in one

(diagrams not to scale) (all measurements approximate)
make two sides equal

Fig. 2a Shoulder notch
Sleeve
5½"
draw line parallel to grain line through shoulder notch, draw curve on each side
6"
mark notch

Trace off each side of sleeve
Fig. 2b
Sleeve Back
Sleeve Front
add seam allowance
centre seam
centre seam

Fig. 4 mark notch
underarm
add seam allowance approx waist
Main Back
trace off main back and then Pin to side front at side seam
trace off side front and pin to main back at side seam
(If side seams are not straight pin together at top and bottom and fill in with paper)

Fig. 3b waist
4"
opening 6"
Pocket Bag
6"
side front seam
make notches at each end of opening
6"

Fig. 3a
Yoke
armhole
yoke seam
mark notches on yoke and front
Pin side seams together
approx waist
draw in yoke seam to run smoothly into armhole, trace off yoke and add seam allowance
Back

Front
enlarge original rever
side front
centre front
5½" 5½"
draw in side front line parallel to centre front add flare lines on each side
cut side front to this line
cut front to this line
draw in front edge in same way as Side front
Cut hem off
4" 4"
5½" 5½"
4"

94

Pressing

On thick wool fabric it is vital to make a well-pressed seam yet not flatten the pile.

Use a very damp cloth and a laundry spray. Press from the wrong side using as much pressure as possible until the seam lies flat. Press again from the wrong side, using plenty of water, but this time very lightly, with the iron only just touching the fabric. The seam will remain sharply pressed but the pile of the fabric will expand or 'lift'.

Bindings

Experiment with the various methods for sewing on bindings shown on page 86 and choose one that is suitable for your fabric.

Making up

Pocket bags Stitch the pocket bags in position on right sides of the side front seams. Press as shown (Fig 6).

Front and back Join the shoulder seams and press open. Bind from the hem up the side front to the shoulder and round the yoke, mitring the point. Bind the

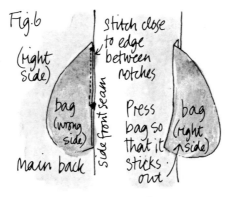

Fig.6 (right side)
Main back
bag (wrong side)
side front seam
stitch close to edge between notches
Press bag so that it sticks out
bag (right side)

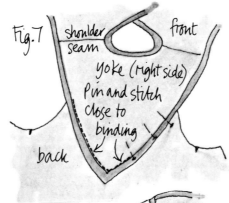

Fig.7
shoulder seam
front
yoke (right side)
Pin and stitch close to binding
back

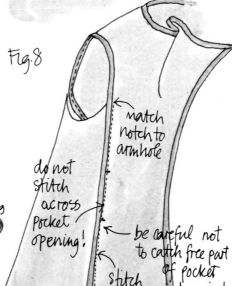

Fig.8
match notch to armhole
do not stitch across pocket opening!
be careful not to catch free part of pocket bag into seams
stitch close to binding

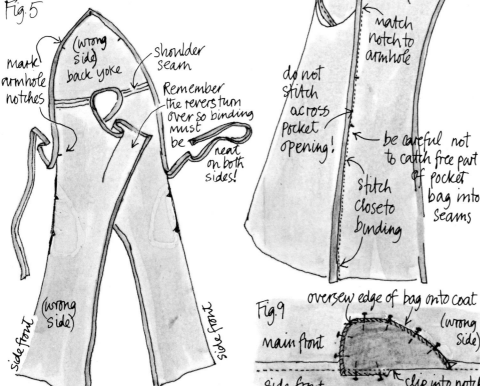

Fig.5
mark armhole notches
(wrong side) back yoke
shoulder seam
Remember the revers turn over so binding must be neat on both sides!
side front
(wrong side)
side front

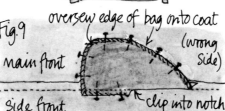

Fig.9
oversew edge of bag onto coat
(wrong side)
main front
side front
clip into notch

front edges, revers and back neck (Fig. 5). Lap the yoke over the back, pin in position and topstitch (Fig. 7).

Lap the fronts over the side front panels and then topstitch in position except between the notches on the pocket bags (Fig. 8). Turn to wrong side and pin the free edges of the pocket bags and stitch (Fig. 9).

Sleeves Bind the front edge of the centre seam. Lap the fronts over the backs, pin and topstitch in position (Fig. 10).
Make the underarm seams, press open and then bind round the wrists.
Pin the sleeves in position under the bound edges of the armholes and topstitch (Fig. 11).
Turn to wrong side and stitch remaining parts of the underarm to the armholes in the usual way. Press.

Finishing off Bind the hem.

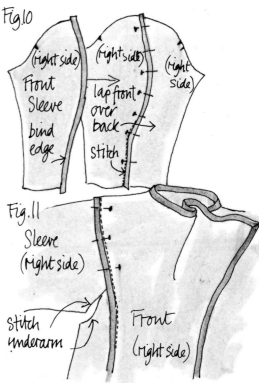

Fig.10
(right side) Front Sleeve bind edge
(right side) lap front over back stitch
(right side)

Fig.11
Sleeve (right side)
stitch underarm
Front (right side)

Variations

Besides the alternatives shown in the instructions, it would be possible to make a similar coat without the side front and yoke seams. Simply bind the revers, back neck, front edges, hem and wrists. This would still allow the facings and hems to be dispensed with, making a coat that would be even easier to sew.

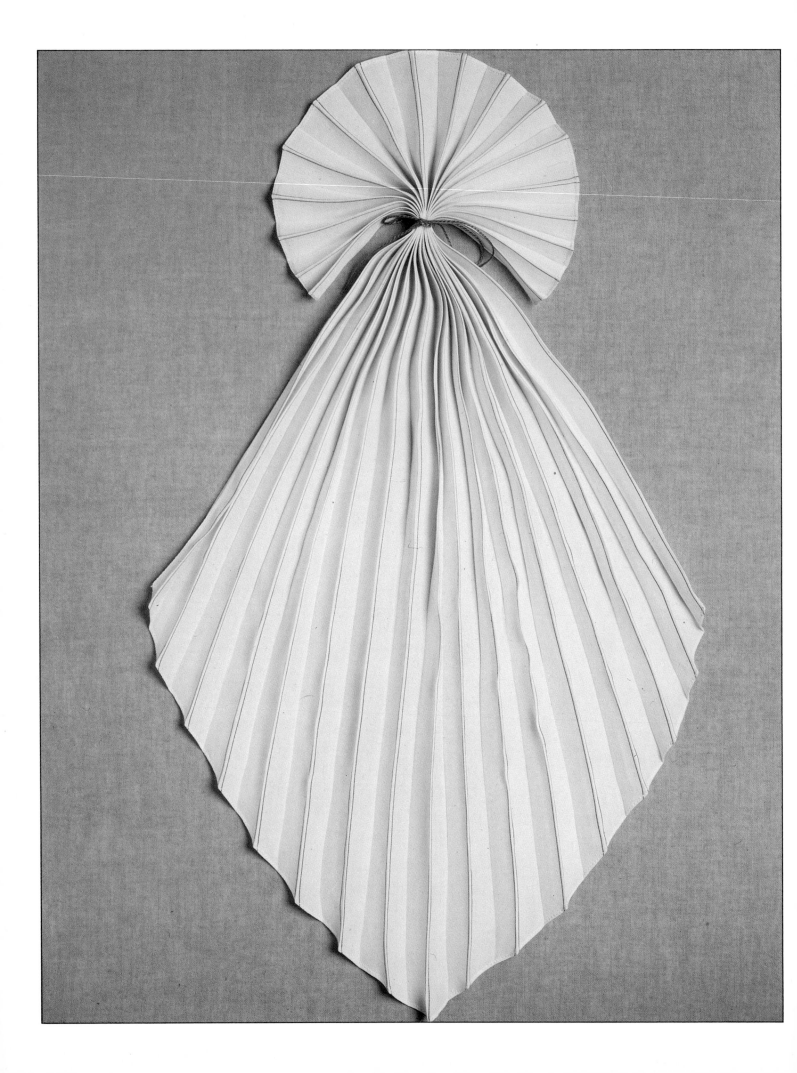

Pleats and Tucks

Dressmakers are often frightened of tucks and pleats; they should not be.
If approached logically and made carefully, they are fairly easy to manage.
The patterns for both are made in a similar way but each is used and stitched quite differently.
Pleats are invariably used vertically and must hang open at one end whereas tucks can be used horizontally or vertically,
and must be closed at both ends – indeed they are usually stitched from end to end. This illustrates
the main difference between the two: tucks are solely decorative, whilst pleats are decorative *and* useful,
as the extra fabric can be utilised where it is needed to allow for movement.
Treat a tuck in the same way and it becomes a pleat, quite a conundrum.
Think of tucks as a row of flaps – useless but pretty.
Contrast that with a few innocent-looking seams opening out
to reveal a flutter of pleats, ready for movement.

◀ *This pleated fan of striped silk is tied with a thread bow.*

Small pleats affect the hem less than large ones

Pleats divide into two categories: pressed and unpressed. This chapter concentrates on the former as they are generally less familiar as a dressmaking technique than the latter; moreover, the method for making the patterns is similar for both. A skirt made with unpressed pleats has a similar soft look to that given by gathers, though they usually hang more elegantly. Pressed pleats on the other hand, give a completely different look; smarter and harder. Both can be used on most types of garment and are certainly not restricted to skirts.

Note: Permanent pleats require special presses to make them, so are not covered here.

Parts of a pleat

It is easiest to start pleating by looking at a single pleat. The constituent parts show up most clearly if this pleat is pressed; it is then called a knife pleat.

It consists of two parts and two folds (or creases):

1 The part which shows, at one edge of which is the outer (or top) fold
2 The part which is hidden, this is divided in half by the inner fold.

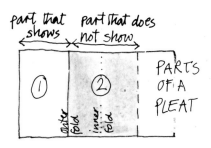

Marking a pleat

Each pleat needs two notches:
★ One to mark the outer fold
★ One to mark how much is folded, or taken into the pleat.
This second notch also shows where the first notch will lie when the pleat is formed.

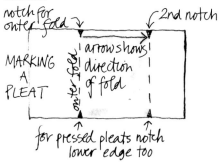

If a pattern is made, an arrow is usually drawn between the two notches to show the direction in which to fold the outer fold.

If the pleats are to be pressed, notches must be made on both the upper and lower edges. It is also useful to draw lines on the pattern between the two sets of notches so that the position of the pleats show clearly. The part between these lines is the part that will be lost inside the pleat.

● NOTE – the inner foldline does not need to be marked with notches as it will appear automatically when the pleat is made.

Making an unpressed pleat

Cut out and clip into the notches. Fold the fabric through the notch for the outer fold, and lay this fold up against the second notch. Pin using two pins to ensure that the upper edge is kept level. Stitch across the pleat close to the upper edge, and again just above the seam allowance.

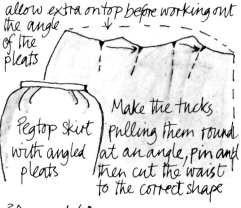

● BEWARE – if the fabric folded into the pleat is allowed to hang out of line at the edge, the pleat will not hang straight. However, this can be exploited to make angled tucks.

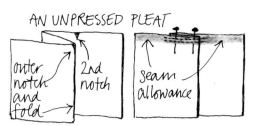

allow extra on top before working out the angle of the pleats

Pegtop skirt with angled pleats

Make the tucks pulling them round at an angle, pin and then cut the waist to the correct shape

Pleated 'straight' skirts from the 30s and 40s

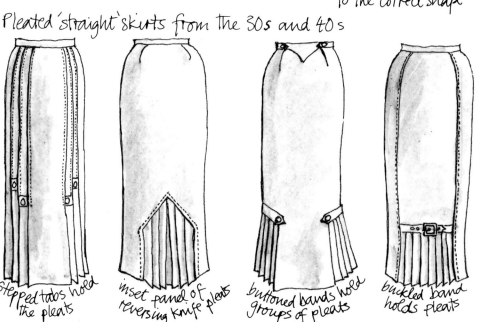

stepped tabs hold the pleats

inset panel of reversing knife pleats

buttoned bands hold groups of pleats

buckled band holds pleats

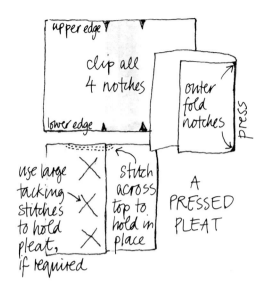

use large tacking stitches to hold pleat, if required

stitch across top to hold in place

upper edge
clip all 4 notches
lower edge

outer fold notches
press

A PRESSED PLEAT

Making a pressed pleat

Cut out and make notches on both the upper and lower edges. Fold the fabric through the outer fold notches and press so that a sharp crease or 'knife' edge is made. Lay this outer fold up against the second pair of notches and pin in place. Turn to the wrong side and press the inner fold. From the right side check that everything looks straight and flat. Pin at each end and stitch across the top edge to hold the pleat in place. If the fabric is difficult to press, or the pleats tend to come out before the garment is finished, it may also be worth tacking them in place.

A second pleat

Measure the amount taken up in the first pleat, mark a third notch to half this width past the second notch, then mark a second pleat in the same way as for the first pleat. Make the pleat as before.

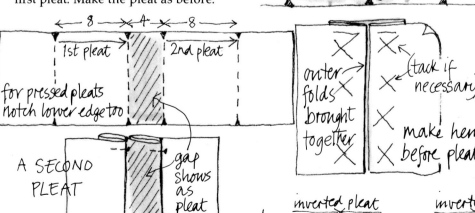

1st pleat 2nd pleat

for pressed pleats notch lower edge too

A SECOND PLEAT

gap shows as pleat

● NOTE – when these two pleats are pinned in place it becomes apparent that it is the gap between the two creases that is seen as the pleat, also that the inner fold lies exactly under the top fold. This is because, in this example, the amount folded into the pleats is exactly twice as much as the distance between them. This gives plenty of fullness and is easy to work out, taking exactly three times the finished measurement.

An inverted pleat

This is done the same way as before except that the marking is different and the pleats are folded to face towards each other. Three notches are needed for each pleat:
★ One for each outer fold
★ One to mark where the outer folds come together.
If a pattern is made, two arrows are drawn to show the direction in which to turn the outer folds.
Fold as shown for knife pleats, then press and tack as shown.
The pleat can now be ignored whilst making up the rest of the garment.

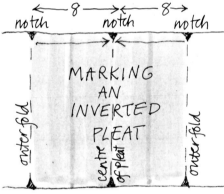

notch 8 notch 8 notch

MARKING AN INVERTED PLEAT

outer fold centre of pleat outer fold

outer folds brought together

(tack if necessary)

make hem before pleat

A second inverted pleat

Measure the amount taken up in one side of the first inverted pleat and mark the second pleat this distance to one side of the first pleat.

● NOTICE – that two inverted pleats made close together automatically form a box pleat between them. Turn the pleats over, the reverse appears: one inverted pleat between two box pleats.

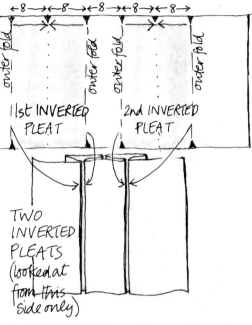

8 8 8 8 8

outer fold outer fold outer fold outer fold

1st INVERTED PLEAT 2nd INVERTED PLEAT

TWO INVERTED PLEATS (looked at from this side only)

● EXPERIMENT – at this stage it would probably be a good idea to mark and pleat up some pieces of paper to make sure exactly how the different types of pleats work. Try out pleats in various widths and with different amounts of fabric taken into them.

● BEWARE – the amount taken into each side of an inverted or box pleat is usually not more than the width of the pleat. Pleats, made in these proportions, are three layers thick. If more fabric is taken into the pleats the result may be too thick and unwieldy.

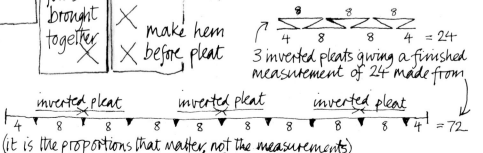

8 8 8
4 8 8 4 = 24

3 inverted pleats giving a finished measurement of 24 made from

inverted pleat inverted pleat inverted pleat

4 8 8 8 8 8 8 8 8 4 = 72

(it is the proportions that matter, not the measurements)

1930s

Dress with horizontal pleats running across neck and continuing onto sleeves

Joining pleats

This is made easy by making joins through the inner folds which of course also means that they do not show. Add seam allowances, make the seams and then press in the pleats. (This method is used for the pleated suit at the end of this chapter.)

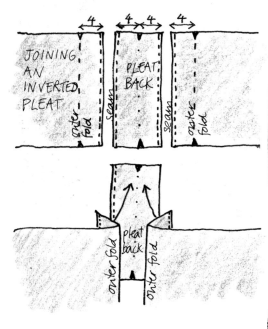

JOINING AN INVERTED PLEAT

● EXPERIMENT – with paper to make sure you understand exactly how the joins work on different sorts of pleats.

Partly stitched pleats

These are often used on the centre back or front of straight skirts but can, of course, be used in other places. Allow extra fabric at the centre – about 2½in. for a knife pleat, 5in. for an inverted pleat.

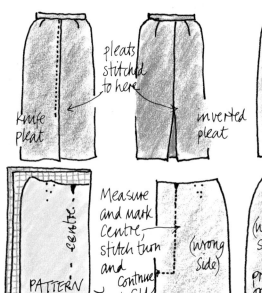

For a knife pleat, press the pleat to one side and continue as illustrated.

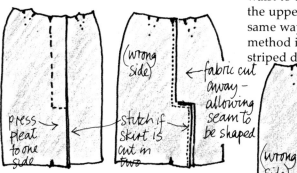

For an inverted pleat, fold and press each side into the centre using the notches at the hem as guides.

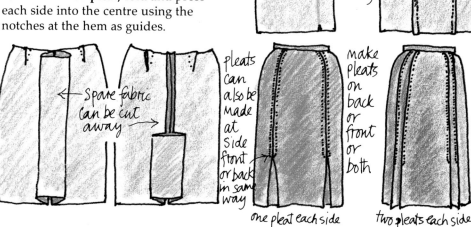

one pleat each side   two pleats each side

Inverted pleat with separate back.

Allow half the amount needed for the pleat at the centre and seam allowances and do not lay to the fold. Also cut a pleat back as shown. Stitch the centre from the

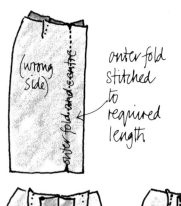

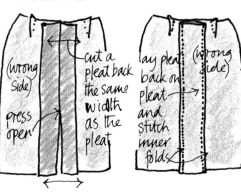

waist to the required depth. Of course the upper part can be cut away in the same way as the knife pleat. (This method is used for the skirt of the striped dress on page 33.)

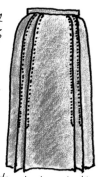

A panoply of pleats! Left: From the French magazine 'Bon Ton', (1921), an afternoon dress with contrast fabric under side pleats to match the collar and cuffs. Top: Fashion student Dorothy Stanson in her Diploma grey flannel (1940s); pleats plus shaped bound edges. Above: A Parisian race-goer (1925) in a matching coat and dress with piped pleats, bands and free-hanging pleats.

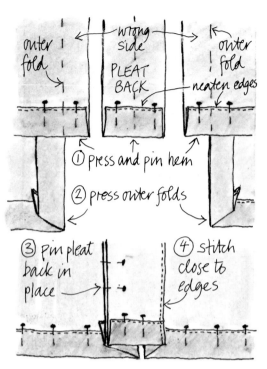

① press and pin hem

② press outer folds

③ pin pleat back in place

④ stitch close to edges

Labels: outer fold, wrong side PLEAT BACK, outer fold, neaten edges

Hems

These pose quite a problem if the pleats are joined through the inner folds. If the amount to be taken up *is* known, the hem can be pressed onto the wrong side before the pleats are made. If the amount to be taken up is *not* known, the last inch of the inner fold seam should be left unstitched until the garment is fitted and the final depth of the hem decided upon.

Fabrics

Almost any fabric can be pleated but only if the right type and size of pleat is used for each particular piece.
Thick or heavy fabrics make beautiful soft unpressed pleats; generally the thicker the fabric, the larger the pleats and therefore the smaller the number needed. More often, though, pleats are made using thinner fabrics; lightweight wools, cottons, silks or linens can all be used to pleat either sharply or softly.
Cloth made from synthetic fibres should be tested before using for pressed pleats as it is often crease-resistant, though if you are determined, this can usually be overcome, either by pressing very hard or by stitching along the edges of the pleats thus holding the creases in place.

Generally soft or loosely woven fabrics do not make good pressed pleats as the creases tend to fall out, so keep to crisper firmer fabrics if sharp edges are required.

● DO – before buying the fabric fold it into pleats, hold it up in front of you and look in a mirror. Does it hang well? How does the pattern (woven or printed) look? Should the pleats be pressed or unpressed? If the fabric is striped, are the stripes straight enough to use as a guide for the pleats?

● BEWARE – printed or woven stripes should be at right angles to the selvedge. Often they are not; nor are they always straight. This makes them useless for any kind of pleat because the pattern of the stripes will end up as a confused jumble.

● REMEMBER – some fabrics hang differently when held up one way or the other (that is with the selvedge vertical or horizontal). See which is best for your purpose.

Washing and pressing

This should suit the fabric being used. If the pleats are complicated, it is better to avoid using a fabric which needs washing often, as re-pressing will take a long time. Pleats generally do not pose any special washing problems, though stitching markers to show the foldlines makes re-pressing quicker. Press from the underside of a pleat, whenever possible, to avoid making impressions on the right side of the garment.

Designing with pleats

Whether used to allow room for movement or to make an interesting detail, pleats tend to give an extravagant air to a garment. Sometimes huge quantities of fabric are hidden in pleats ready to swirl out when moved; more often the amount of extra fabric is small, but nonetheless effective.

Pleats can be inserted almost anywhere as long as the necessary extra amount is allowed in the pattern, or for simple garments, when cutting the fabric.
It is also necessary to consider how the pleats will hang. This is largely a matter of gravity; they will always tend to hang

1930s — self-striped mousseline silk — fabric pleated to expose satin stripes

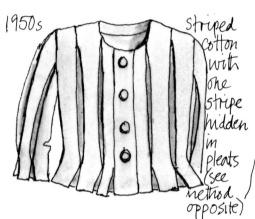

1950s — striped cotton with one stripe hidden in pleats (see method opposite)

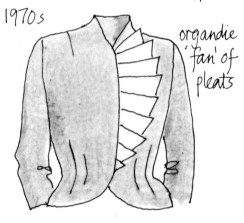

1970s — organdie 'fan' of pleats

vertically if they are open at the lower end. Pleats used horizontally tend to fall open, and for this reason are generally stitched, in which case they are usually considered to be tucks rather than pleats. Restraining pleats in some places and leaving them open in others means they can be used to allow ease or room for movement.
Mark lines for the pleats, split the pattern through these lines and spread apart by the required amount. Fold the pleats into the pattern, pin and cut out.

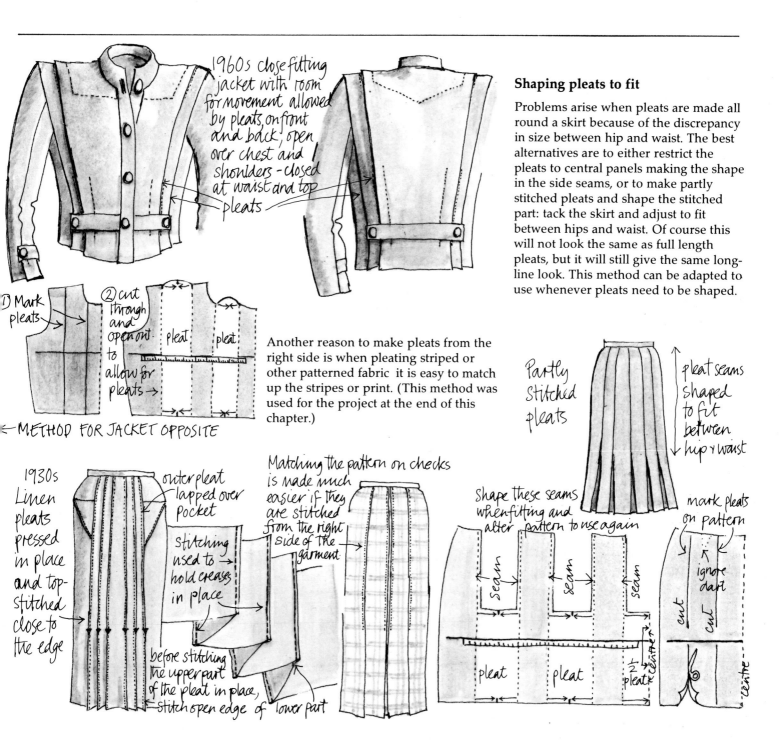

1960s close fitting jacket with room for movement allowed by pleats on front and back, open over chest and shoulders - closed at waist and top pleats

1) Mark pleats

2) cut through and open out to allow for pleats

pleat   pleat

← METHOD FOR JACKET OPPOSITE

1930s Linen pleats pressed in place and top-stitched close to the edge

outer pleat lapped over pocket

Stitching used to hold creases in place

before stitching the upper part of the pleat in place, stitch open edge of lower part

Another reason to make pleats from the right side is when pleating striped or other patterned fabric it is easy to match up the stripes or print. (This method was used for the project at the end of this chapter.)

Matching the pattern on checks is made much easier if they are stitched from the right side of the garment.

Shaping pleats to fit

Problems arise when pleats are made all round a skirt because of the discrepancy in size between hip and waist. The best alternatives are to either restrict the pleats to central panels making the shape in the side seams, or to make partly stitched pleats and shape the stitched part: tack the skirt and adjust to fit between hips and waist. Of course this will not look the same as full length pleats, but it will still give the same long-line look. This method can be adapted to use whenever pleats need to be shaped.

Partly Stitched pleats

pleat seams shaped to fit between hip & waist

Shape these seams when fitting and alter pattern to use again

seam   seam   seam

pleat   pleat   ½ pleat

mark pleats on pattern

ignore dart

cut   cut

centre

An easy method is to stitch the pleats entirely from the right side by pressing them into position and topstitching close to the edge of the outer folds. Sometimes the free lower part of the outer fold is stitched too, either for decoration or to hold the crease. If done for the latter reason, the inner fold is often stitched in the same way. This was a common device before the days of permanent pleating and is still useful nowadays when a washable fabric is used for pleating.

To make unpressed pleats all round a skirt

Measure the hips – say 38in. Decide on the width of the pleats – say 2in. = 19 pleats.
Cut a piece of fabric – 3 x 38in. + 1½in. (seam) wide = 115in. – by the required length, + hem + seam. Notch the waist. Make the pleats as described before.

Making pleats is one of the most satisfying dressmaking techniques. The effect a single pleat can have is out of all proportion to the small amount of extra work involved. So start with just one pleat and work through this chapter, by which time you should be able to produce a positive panoply of pleats. (For further examples of pattern cutting with pleats see page 138.)

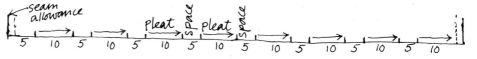

seam allowance

Pleat   space   Pleat   space

5   10   5   10   5   10   5   10   5   10   5   10   5   10   5   10

Nothing could demonstrate more clearly the dichotomy between tucks and pleats than this suit. The skirt could be said to be pleated, but what of the jacket, especially the sleeves? Are these tucks, or pleats? No matter. The jacket is almost entirely made from unstitched pleats – or tucks if you like – held in place by the shoulder bands, restrained by the facings and hanging free at the hem, (except those on the sleeves which are held in place by the underarm seams) (Fig. 1).

The skirt has flat, buttoned front bands and a flat back band to match the jacket. The pleats on the skirt echo those on the jacket except that they are stitched to just below hip level.

The intricate appearance of this suit does not mean that it is difficult, but it does take time and much patience to press in all the pleats. Not something to run up in an evening.

Fabric

A firm twilled cotton of a similar weight to ordinary poplin is used for the suit. Thicker fabrics could be used to make a heavier outfit, but whatever is chosen, it must press sharply. Aim for a fabric with a simple, fairly wide stripe and not too large a repeat. Experiment with the pleats before buying , to get some idea of how a particular stripe might look and how much fabric will be taken up. The sample shown used 5½yds of fabric, 60in.

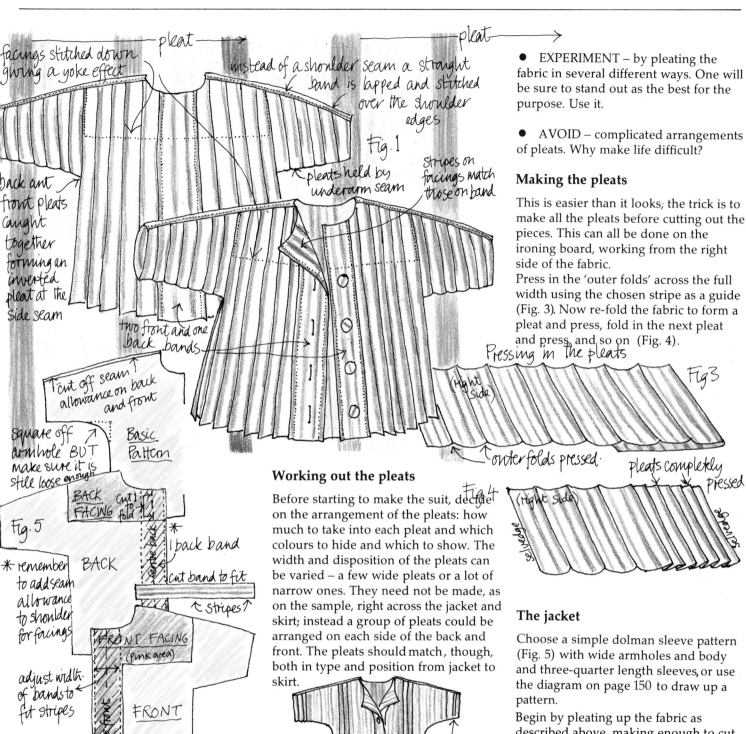

Fig. 1 — facings stitched down giving a yoke effect · pleat · instead of a shoulder seam a straight band is lapped and stitched over the shoulder edges · back and front pleats caught together forming an inverted pleat at the side seam · pleats held by underarm seam · stripes on facings match those on band · two front and one back bands

Fig. 2 — Alternative arrangement for pleats — less work, less fabric · pleats

Fig. 5 (Basic Pattern) — cut off seam allowance on back and front · square off armhole BUT make sure it is still loose enough · BACK FACING, cut 1 to fold · BACK · 1 back band · cut band to fit · stripes · remember to add seam allowance to shoulder for facings · FRONT FACING (pink area) · adjust width of bands to fit stripes · FRONT · centre front · 2 front bands

Fig. 3 — Pressing in the pleats · (right side) · outer folds pressed

Fig. 4 — (right side) · selvedge · pleats completely pressed · selvedge

- EXPERIMENT – by pleating the fabric in several different ways. One will be sure to stand out as the best for the purpose. Use it.

- AVOID – complicated arrangements of pleats. Why make life difficult?

Making the pleats

This is easier than it looks; the trick is to make all the pleats before cutting out the pieces. This can all be done on the ironing board, working from the right side of the fabric.

Press in the 'outer folds' across the full width using the chosen stripe as a guide (Fig. 3). Now re-fold the fabric to form a pleat and press, fold in the next pleat and press, and so on (Fig. 4).

Working out the pleats

Before starting to make the suit, decide on the arrangement of the pleats: how much to take into each pleat and which colours to hide and which to show. The width and disposition of the pleats can be varied – a few wide pleats or a lot of narrow ones. They need not be made, as on the sample, right across the jacket and skirt; instead a group of pleats could be arranged on each side of the back and front. The pleats should match, though, both in type and position from jacket to skirt.

The jacket

Choose a simple dolman sleeve pattern (Fig. 5) with wide armholes and body and three-quarter length sleeves, or use the diagram on page 150 to draw up a pattern.

Begin by pleating up the fabric as described above, making enough to cut out the entire jacket. This can be done in one length or cut into four pieces, (Figs 6 and 7 overpage).

Cut out

From the pleated fabric:
1 pair fronts (including 2 bands)
1 pair backs (including 1 band only)
Pin all the pleats in place, at each end.
From unpleated flat fabric (remembering to add seam allowances to shoulders):

wide. The jacket used four widths, the skirt two. The pleats took up three times their finished width. It might also be a good idea to read the chapter on stripes.

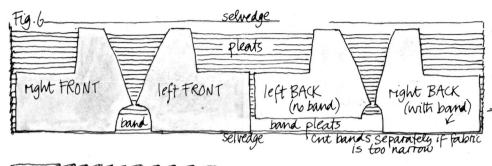

Fig. 6

selvedge

pleats

right FRONT | left FRONT | left BACK (no band) | right BACK (with band)

band

band pleats

selvedge

cut bands separately if fabric is too narrow

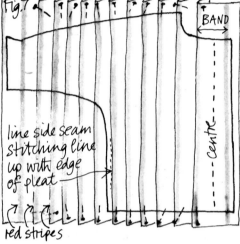

Fig. 7

BAND

line side seam stitching line up with edge of pleat

centre

red stripes

1 pair fronts facings (cut to match the stripes on the front bands)
1 back neck facing (cut to the fold at the centre back)
1 pair shoulder bands

Making up

Stitch the pleats in place on the shoulders and underarms close to the edge. (Fig. 8).
Press the seam allowances on the shoulder bands to the wrong side.
Lay out the backs and fronts, right side up, so that the shoulders come together.
Lap the shoulder bands centrally over the shoulder edges, pin and topstitch close to the edge (or just inside the edge stripe if the fabric used is similar to that in the sample (Fig. 8).

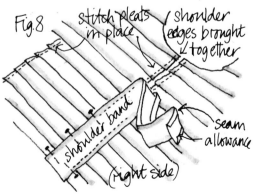

Fig. 8

stitch pleats in place

shoulder edges brought together

shoulder band

seam allowance

(right side)

Pin the back band in place on the other side of the back and topstitch to match the shoulder band (Fig. 9).
Stitch front bands similarly (Fig. 10).
Join the facings at the shoulder seams (Fig. 11).

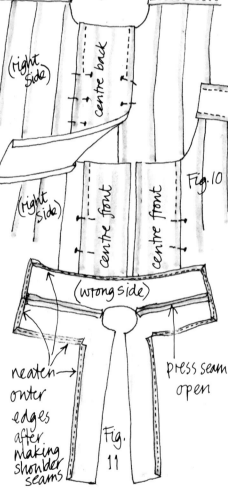

Fig. 9

(right side)

centre back

(right side)

centre front | centre front

Fig. 10

(wrong side)

neaten outer edges after making shoulder seams

press seam open

Fig. 11

Pin in place on the main jacket, right sides together. Stitch round the neck and along front edges. Press the facing onto the wrong side.
Pin the outer free edges of the facing in place, keeping it flat, and stitch across the lower edge of the back, turning at the

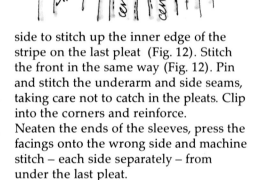

Fig. 12

Stitch facing through onto main pieces to hold pleats

centre back

carry stitching across bands

(right side)

centre front | centre front

side to stitch up the inner edge of the stripe on the last pleat (Fig. 12). Stitch the front in the same way (Fig. 12). Pin and stitch the underarm and side seams, taking care not to catch in the pleats. Clip into the corners and reinforce.
Neaten the ends of the sleeves, press the facings onto the wrong side and machine stitch – each side separately – from under the last pleat.

The skirt

No pattern is needed as the skirt is completely straight – a sort of pleated tube when buttoned up – though a little shape is made at the waist (Fig. 13).
The sample is very long: 32in. finished, worn by a model 5′ 8″ tall. It should be made to fit loosely over the hips, so measure and add about 2in. to allow for ease.

Cut out

Enough widths of fabric to give approximately three times this measurement. For example, for 38in. hips, add 2in.: 100 x 3 = 120in.
Of course the skirt can be made with fewer pleats, so taking less fabric, but if made with too few the whole effect – of a tube over the hips with swirling fullness below – will be lost.
Two widths of 36in. wide fabric plus extra for the bands would be about the minimum to gain this effect.
Cut the fabric as shown in Fig. 14. Also cut two front facings for the bands.

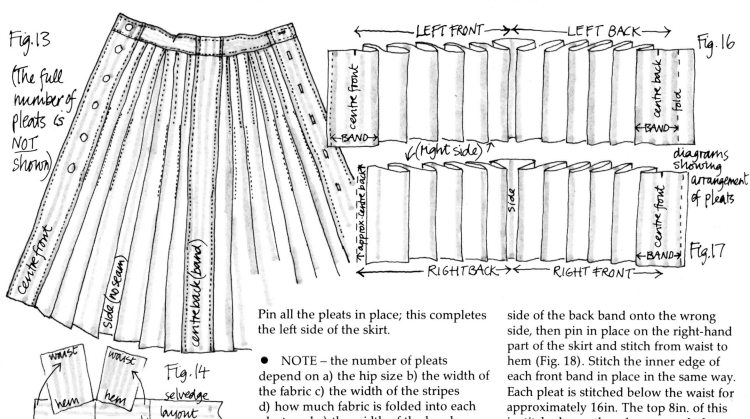

Fig. 13 (The full number of pleats is NOT shown)

Labels on Fig.13: centre front, side (no seam), centre back (band)

Fig. 14 selvedge layout showing how to reverse the stripes selvedge

Labels: waist, waist, hem, hem, waist, hem, hem, waist

Fig. 16 LEFT FRONT — LEFT BACK — centre front, BAND, centre back fold, (right side)

Fig. 17 diagrams showing arrangement of pleats — approx. centre back, side, centre front, BAND, RIGHT BACK — RIGHT FRONT

Making up

Start by forming the left front band by pressing in a pleat at the left of one piece (Fig. 15). This pleat is only different from the ensuing pleats in that it is stitched down from waist to hem, but do this after the remaining pleats are made. Press in enough pleats to give half the finished hip measurement, less the width of the band.
Join in further widths of fabric if necessary, through inner folds (with pins at this stage), keeping the pattern of the stripes correct.
The pleats should turn at the centre to face in the opposite direction, forming an inverted pleat on the side.
Finish by forming a back band in the same way, but in reverse, as on the front band (Fig. 16).

Fig. 15 width of BAND, outer fold (right side), LEFT FRONT

Pin all the pleats in place; this completes the left side of the skirt.

● NOTE – the number of pleats depend on a) the hip size b) the width of the fabric c) the width of the stripes d) how much fabric is folded into each pleat, and e) the width of the bands.

Make the right-hand side of the skirt in the same way. The only difference is that there is no back band, so start with the pleats for the right back and continue round, working in reverse ending up with the right front band (Fig. 17).
Pin all the pleats in place; this completes the right side of the skirt.

Making up the skirt

Press the half pleat on the right-hand

Fig. 18 (right side), BACK BAND, trim edge to match, LEFT BACK, top stitch each side, RIGHT BACK

Fig. 19 measure pleats pin and stitch, (right side)

side of the back band onto the wrong side, then pin in place on the right-hand part of the skirt and stitch from waist to hem (Fig. 18). Stitch the inner edge of each front band in place in the same way. Each pleat is stitched below the waist for approximately 16in. The top 8in. of this is stitched near the edge to match the bands, and the lower 8in. is stitched at the inner edge of the pleat (Fig. 19). To do this: measure the pleats, from the outer fold to the inner fold and stitch each one this distance from the edge, starting 8in. below the waist and continuing for another 8in. This allows this lower part of the pleat to flap free (see detail page 104). (If you prefer a flatter look, stitch each pleat for the full 16in. as described for the upper part.) The upper part of the pleats can now be shaped in to fit the waist. Unpin the top 6in. of each pleat and try the skirt on, pinning the right-hand front band to lap exactly over the left-hand front band. Smooth in the pleats on each side, front and back, so that they shape in to fit the waist. In other words, each pleat is lapped over a little more than before, thus curving in gently to fit at the waist (Fig. 13). Take the skirt off, check that each side is the same and then stitch the pleats from the waist down, finishing where the lower stitching begins (Fig. 13).
Face the front bands.
Set on the waistband.
Make buttonholes and sew on buttons.
Make the hem, referring to the notes on hems in the first part of the chapter.

Ruching

In most people's imagery, ruching is entirely represented by red velvet theatre curtains
hanging in softly scalloped rows ready to be gathered upwards when the performance begins.
The Victorian dressmaker loved ruching, both for the ease with which it could be used,
and for the somewhat rococo results. Needless to say,
they overdid it, covering hats, dresses, curtains and lampshades with multiple
bands of ruching, often further embellished with lace and frills.
As usual the designers of the 30s did it better. They used ruching cleverly,
either as part of the structure of a garment, giving shape to sensuous satin and crêpe dresses,
or more discreetly as decoration on otherwise plain garments.
By the 50s the 'New Look' had changed our shape, requiring much more emphasis on the bust;
ruching worked hard flattering the perfect figure or hiding the embarrassment of both the
under and over-endowed. The 60s and 70s gave the technique a well-needed rest,
from which it has emerged as fuel for the current 'crumpled' look.

panné velvet   1930s   grosgrain

◄ *Silk organza ruched by a form of smocking.*

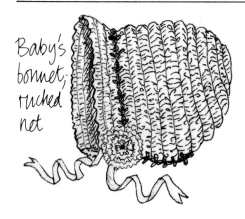

Baby's bonnet, ruched net

The word 'ruching' describes any method of holding fabric in folds or 'ruches', right across its width. This is usually done by means of rows of gathering stitches but nowadays is also done with irregular tucks.

● NOTE – 'ruching', 'shirring' and 'draping' occasionally overlap in effect but they are three quite distinct techniques. Draping is much more complicated than ruching and is usually done on a dressmaker's dummy, whilst shirring uses elastic to make the gathers.

There are three principal ways of ruching:

1 Gather up (or tuck) both edges – this is the most widely used method as it is the most versatile, especially when made into long narrow strips which can then be applied, straight or curved, as

decoration. Alternatively they can be inset, thus becoming part of the structure of the garment.

2 Gather or tuck one long edge, leaving the other edge flat, in which case the whole piece will curve. It is still easy to sew, but cutting the pattern is more complicated. This method is generally used for one-sided effects, though it can just as well be used on both sides of a central seam. In either case the fullness can be utilised to give shape, or not, as required.

3 Occasionally a piece is gathered or ruched down the centre, without a seam. This is a fairly limited method, mostly used at the centre front of bodices and skirts to give shape. An offshoot of this is using a drawstring, or elastic, to give a ruched effect.

To make a ruched strip, cut a long strip of fabric, run gathers (or tucks) along both long edges and draw them up. The strip can then be curved by tightening one side more than the other, or made to wave by pulling up the gathers alternately tighter and looser.

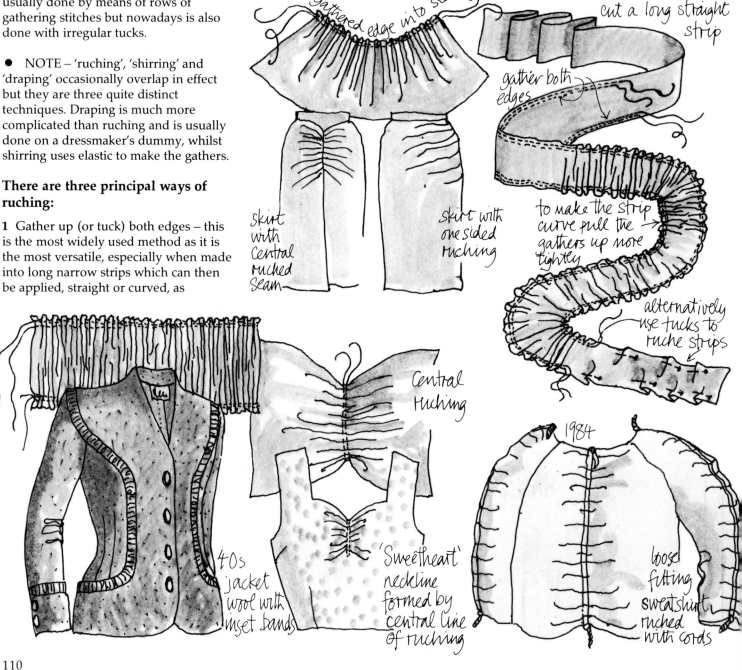

set gathered edge into seam

skirt with central ruched seam

skirt with one sided ruching

cut a long straight strip

gather both edges

to make the strip curve pull the gathers up more tightly

alternatively use tucks to ruche strips

40s jacket wool with inset bands

central ruching

'Sweetheart' neckline formed by central line of ruching

1984

loose fitting sweatshirt ruched with cords

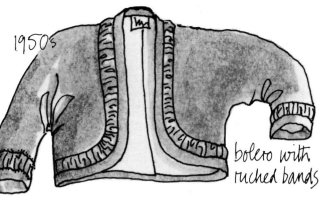

1950s

bolero with ruched bands

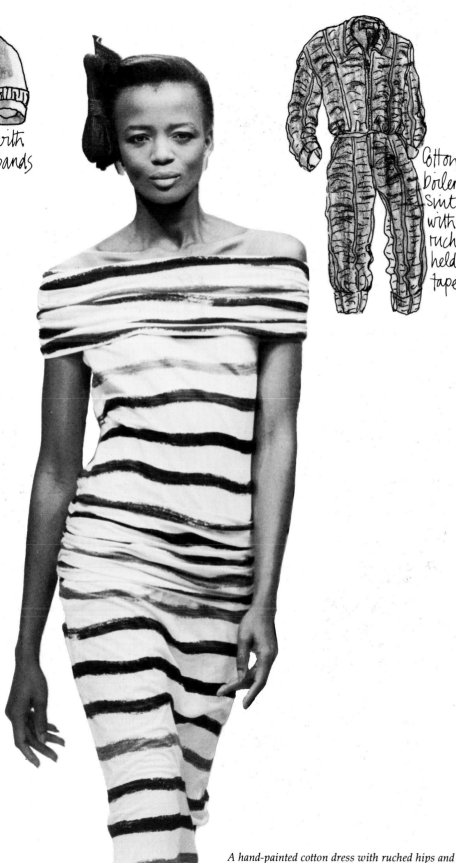

Cotton boiler suit with ruching held by tapes

The amount of fabric to allow

This depends on both the fabric and whether you want it tightly or only slightly ruched. Experiment with the amount of gathers needed. Some fabrics may need a lot of extra material or they will look skimped; others will look good whether slightly or fully ruched. Start with about one and a half times the finished length (using ordinary woven cottons, for example). For a strip 20in. long, cut the piece 30in. long.
Some fine materials such as muslin may need as much as three times the finished length. Generally the thicker the fabric the less fullness needed.

● DO NOT WORRY – about the gathers being even all the way along the strip. It is fairly easy to adjust them to look even (which is what matters) by eye.

● BEWARE – some fabrics gather quite differently if cut along the warp than if cut along the weft, usually because these are noticeably different, thus causing the gathers to either puff out or flute narrowly. Try strips cut in both directions from one material to see whether they look different; if they do, choose the one most suitable for your purpose.

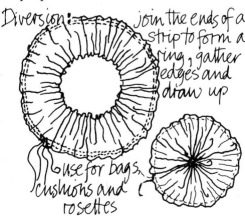

Diversion: join the ends of a strip to form a ring, gather edges and draw up

use for bags, cushions and rosettes

A hand-painted cotton dress with ruched hips and shoulder band, by the French designer Lanvin, 1984. A very simple design to copy.

111

Left: A green silk shift by Ungaro, 1984, with ruched skirt and sleeves. Top: A 1930s or early 1940s knitting pattern by Patons & Baldwins, showing that even knitting can be ruched! Above: A French ballgown dated 1862 with fine ruching and frills.

Altering the pattern

For set-in bands, mark the position and width of the band on the pattern. Trace off each piece. Measure the longest edge and cut the band to this length, plus half

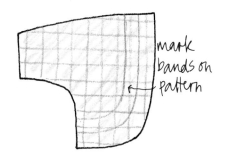

mark bands on pattern

as much again for the gathers; measure the width and add seam allowances.

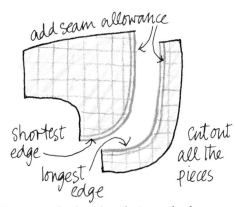

add seam allowance

shortest edge

longest edge

Cut out all the pieces

Draw up the band and pin to the longer edge; adjust to fit and arrange the gathers evenly. Stitch with the flat side on top so that the gathers are not pushed out of position.

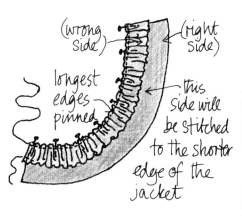

(wrong side)   (right side)

longest edges pinned

this side will be stitched to the shorter edge of the jacket

Pin the second side to the shorter edge, again drawing up the gathers to fit and checking that they appear even. Stitch. Press the seam allowances under the flat side.

For large shaped pieces, lay the pattern on a piece of paper and draw round, up to where the ruching is to start. Decide how much fabric needs to be taken up into the ruching; mark this amount above the top. Complete the pattern as shown.

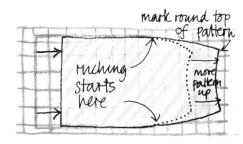

mark round top of pattern

ruching starts here

more pattern up

For a one-sided ruche, proceed as before but allowing the extra on one side only, shaping the waist (or any other relevant part) down to the original pattern as shown. This method is only suitable when small amounts of ruching are required.

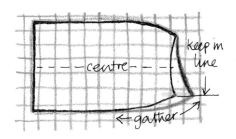

centre

keep in line

gather

● NOTE – this will often make the waist larger than the original. The extra is usually taken up with small tucks or gathers which will be more or less hidden by the ruching.

For one-sided ruching where a lot of fullness is required, draw lines across the pattern where it is to be ruched. Cut through the lines almost to the flat side.

Lay the pattern on a sheet of paper and open out the cuts to allow the extra amount required for the gathers. Draw round the pattern making a smooth curve on the gathered edge.

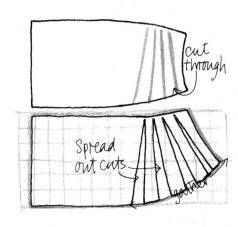

cut through

spread out cuts

gather

This method can also be used for ruching running from a central seam or dart.

Many different versions can be worked using these principles but some adjustments may be necessary when fitting, though these are usually too minor to need a preparatory toile, unless a difficult or expensive fabric is used.

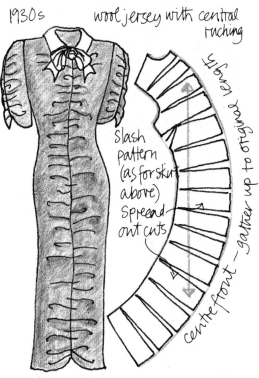

1930s   wool jersey with central ruching

Slash pattern (as for skirt above) spread out cuts

centre front – gather up to original length

113

Extending paper patterns for ruching

To ruche a camisole dress, use a paper pattern like the one illustrated. Lay the pattern on the fabric (or paper if you want to make a new pattern). Mark the hem and up to the hip. Add however much is needed for the ruching above the top. Move the pattern up and draw round the top edge. Draw in the sides so that the extra length is proportioned out evenly from hem to hip, hip to waist and waist to top. Make seams at the centre front and back, adding seam allowances.

To ruche a blouse, begin by working out how much extra is needed for the gathers – the original Edwardian ones were often very full and used about three times the finished length. Mark the neck and armhole bands on a suitable bodice block. Cut straight bands for these, three times as long as the longest edge. Trace off the curved bands, adding seam allowances, to use as facing patterns.

Trace off the main piece and make marks on the edges as shown; lay on a large folded sheet of pattern paper. Draw from the centre to the first mark and measure

and draw from the first mark to the second. Again move the pattern over by three times this amount. Continue right across the pattern.

Cut out in fabric and gather up to fit the original pattern. Sew on the ruched neck and armhole bands (the seams could be trimmed with piping or braid), and then sew on the facings which will, apart from neatening the edges, hold the ruches firmly in place.

Seams

The only problems with seaming ruching is excess bulk.

★ Where the ruched edge is going to be joined to a flat edge, it is probably best to make an ordinary seam. Sometimes, when the ruched fabric is thick, it is worth trimming back the seam allowances on the flat edge. Do this after

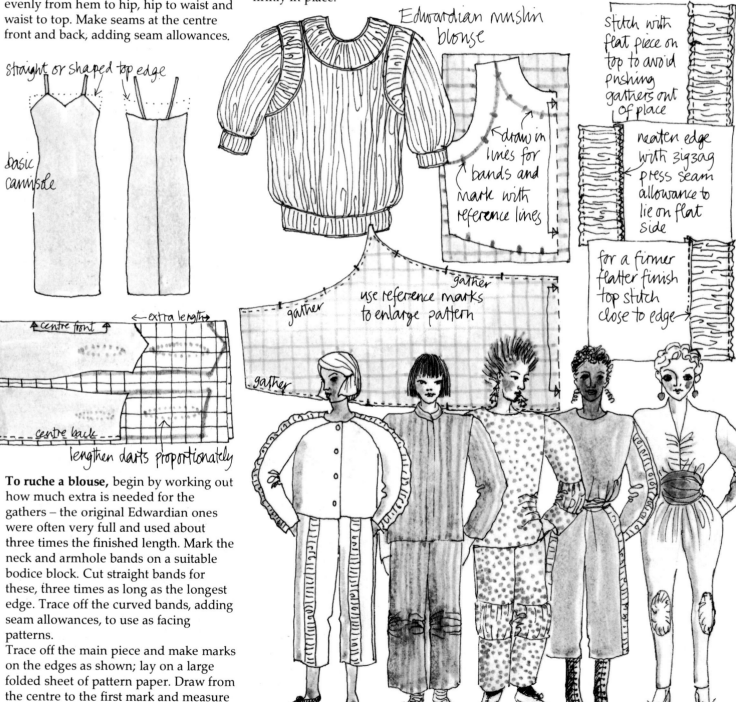

straight or shaped top edge

basic camisole

Edwardian muslin blouse

draw in lines for bands and mark with reference lines

centre front

extra length

lengthen darts proportionately

centre back

gather

gather

gather

use reference marks to enlarge pattern

stitch with flat piece on top to avoid pushing gathers out of place

neaten edge with zigzag press seam allowance to lie on flat side

for a firmer flatter finish top stitch close to edge

sewing the seam so that it is narrower than the ruched side of the seam and then neaten the edge separately.

● AVOID – narrow seam allowances as the edge of the ruched piece is liable to become irregular and might need to be trimmed.

★ When two ruched edges are to be joined, use an ordinary seam but neaten the edges separately and then press the seam allowances open. Of course, this is more bulky than a one-sided ruche, so consider the fabric you use carefully.

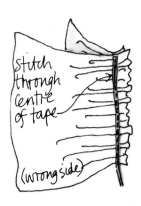

stitch through centre of tape

(wrong side)

★ On fine or stretchy fabrics, when both sides are ruched, a narrow stay tape can be stitched into the seam to stop it stretching or tearing. Use the narrowest, thinnest tape you can find for this or it will make the seam lumpy.

The use of new fabrics, not traditionally used for ruching has given rise to

Ruching a seam with elastic:

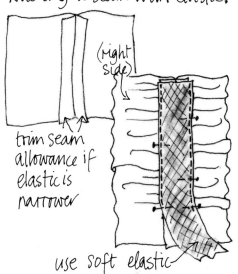

(right side)

trim seam allowance if elastic is narrower

use soft elastic

various new methods of making seams. These can, of course, also be used with the traditional fabrics.

1 Before ruching the seam, stitch it the wrong side out (that is, with the seam allowance lying on the right side). Press open.
Cut a piece of elastic (unstretched) to the finished length of the seam and pin on the right side. Backstitch over the end, stretch out the elastic, pin and stitch over the seam a little way, and continue in this way until the end. Stitch the second side. This requires practice and care to achieve an evenly ruched effect.

2 Make the seam with a large stitch and then draw up the stitching to make gathers. It is probably a good idea to stitch a second row, of normal size, to hold the gathers, which otherwise might break if any strain is put on them.

taping a ruched seam:

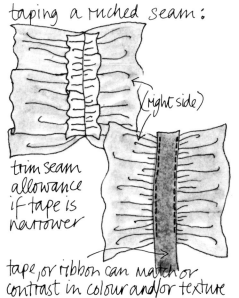

(right side)

trim seam allowance if tape is narrower

tape, or ribbon can match or contrast in colour and/or texture

3 Make the seam, again with large stitches, but the wrong way out. Draw up to make gathers, lay tape or ribbon over the seam and stitch along both edges, thus hiding the raw edges – useful where both sides show.

Fabrics

Anything which gathers well will ruche well. Crêpe–backed satins and lamés were the favourites of the 30s and 40s for evening clothes, plainer crêpes for daywear. Nowadays we can add the modern jersey fabrics made from natural and synthetic fibres.

Fabrics can be mixed; for example, a thin material ruched and set into a similarly textured but much thicker one. Or contrasting textures can be juxtaposed – try crisp shiny taffeta with soft wool, and transparent fabrics, such as nets, chiffon or gauze, ruched and set into opaque materials, to reveal gleams of flesh. Show off the sheen of satin, velvet and other shiny materials by ruching, but be careful with the stiffer ones as they can sometimes look like crumpled paper – though used in the right place this too can look effective.

● EXPERIMENT – with soft fabrics, both knitted and woven. Try brushed sweat-shirting or single cotton jersey, perhaps ruched by means of tucks instead of gathers, a method I have seen used successfully with denim to make ruched jeans.

● REMEMBER – it is obviously very difficult to press ruched fabrics, so any material that is used should either be dry-cleaned or should not crumple or crease, if washed, more than modern fashion considers acceptable.

Pressing ruching

The fabric should be pressed well after cutting out but before drawing up the gathers because, as mentioned above, it is often impossible to press after ruching, especially on small pieces. The seams should be pressed from the wrong side in the usual way.

1940s printed muslin

ruching

115

Designing with ruching

Almost anything that can be sewn together can incorporate ruching. The few fabrics that are unsuitable can be decorated with ruched strips or insets of another fabric.

Try ruched yokes and bibs on shirts and dresses; try ruched pockets, plackets, even pelmets. Eye every seam; maybe ruching it would be the way to give a simple garment an interesting detail. Or set wider bands into a garment to become part of the structure, the added fullness being utilised for movement.

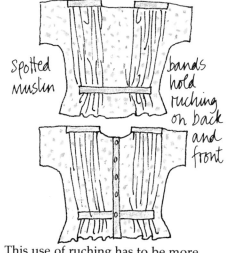

Spotted muslin — bands hold ruching on back and front

This use of ruching has to be more carefully thought out when designing, but if kept simple is not too difficult to manage.

When a thorough understanding of the use of inset bands is achieved, more complicated shapes become easier to work out. It would probably be best to make a toile (or rough) in such cases to make sure a design works, adjusting it until the pattern is perfect. Choose a fairly simple shape and consider several alternative designs. Large ruched areas are more likely to need adjustments than small areas as the fullness is less controlled.

● REMEMBER – to make some sort of adjustment to the design so that the front

and back of the garment relate to each other.

If a ruched garment is worn so that it fits closely, the gathers will tend to form neat folds more or less at right angles to the stitching. On the other hand, if cut to fit loosely, the gathers will tend to hang in loops and a scalloped effect appear at the hem. This is a general principle and varies with the fabric used, but usually the looser a garment is, the greater the scalloped effect will be.

Ruched areas lapped round the sides or shoulders will, if the garment is loosely cut, fall into beautiful softly looped folds, as the project that follows illustrates.

Ruching is such a seductive technique that you will probably find you want to use it for everything – trousers, bags, cushions and lampshades, as well as dresses. Oh dear, back to the Victorians!

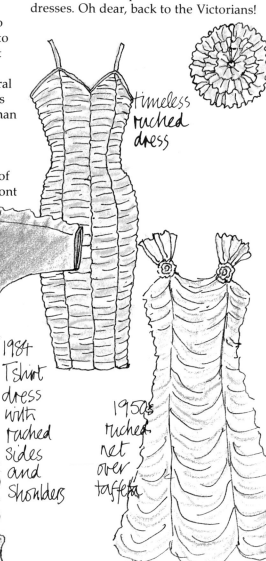

timeless ruched dress

1950s ruched net over taffeta

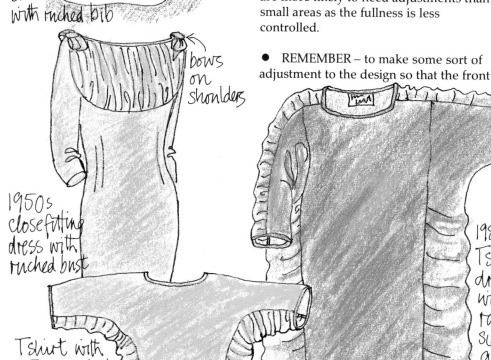

dress shirt with ruched bib

bows on shoulders

1950s closefitting dress with ruched bust

Tshirt with ruched sides

1984 Tshirt dress with ruched sides and shoulders

The ruching on this dress is held by a 'V' shaped band, thus reversing the usual principle of ruching design. The softly scalloped folds around the sides show off the satin's sheen, while making an unusual silhouette which will flatter – if only by concealing – most figures. Choose a simple dolman sleeve shift pattern with sleeves that end just above the elbow, a wide neckline, and the back similar to the front (Fig. 1). Alternatively, use the pattern diagram given on page 151.

Adapting the pattern

Draw a 'V' shape on the pattern as shown in Fig. 2, and trace off the three parts onto separate pieces of paper. The central triangle and the main part must now be extended to allow for the ruching (Figs 3 and 4). Add seam allowances to the centre and both long edges of the 'V' shaped piece. Cut out the pattern pieces (Fig. 5).

Fabric

The sample shown was made from a very soft and pliable silk satin. A successful toile was made first, in a white cotton crêpe. So, any thin soft fabric which gathers and hangs well could be used.

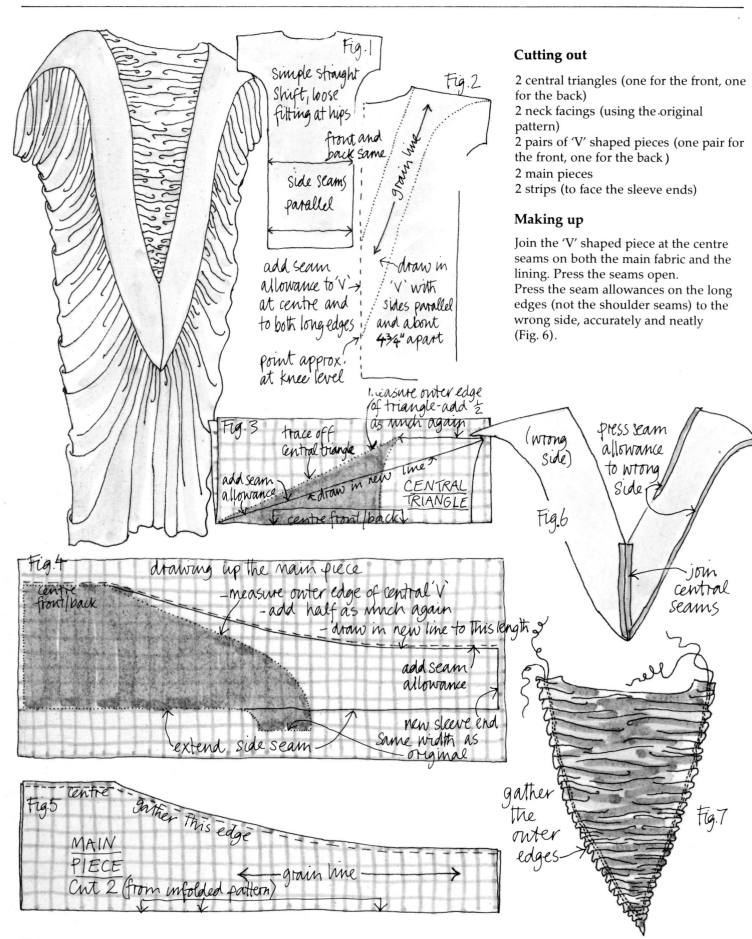

Cutting out

2 central triangles (one for the front, one for the back)
2 neck facings (using the original pattern)
2 pairs of 'V' shaped pieces (one pair for the front, one pair for the back)
2 main pieces
2 strips (to face the sleeve ends)

Making up

Join the 'V' shaped piece at the centre seams on both the main fabric and the lining. Press the seams open.
Press the seam allowances on the long edges (not the shoulder seams) to the wrong side, accurately and neatly (Fig. 6).

Fig. 1 Simple straight shift, loose fitting at hips. front and back same. side seams parallel. add seam allowance to 'V' at centre and to both long edges. point approx. at knee level.

Fig. 2 grain line. draw in 'V' with sides parallel and about 4¾" apart.

Fig. 3 trace off central triangle. measure outer edge of triangle - add ½ as much again. add seam allowance. draw in new line. CENTRAL TRIANGLE. centre front/back.

Fig. 4 drawing up the main piece. centre front/back. — measure outer edge of central 'V' — add half as much again — draw in new line to this length. add seam allowance. extend side seam. new sleeve end same width as original.

Fig. 5 centre. gather this edge. MAIN PIECE. Cut 2 (from unfolded pattern). grain line.

Fig. 6 (wrong side). press seam allowance to wrong side. join central seams.

Fig. 7 gather the outer edges.

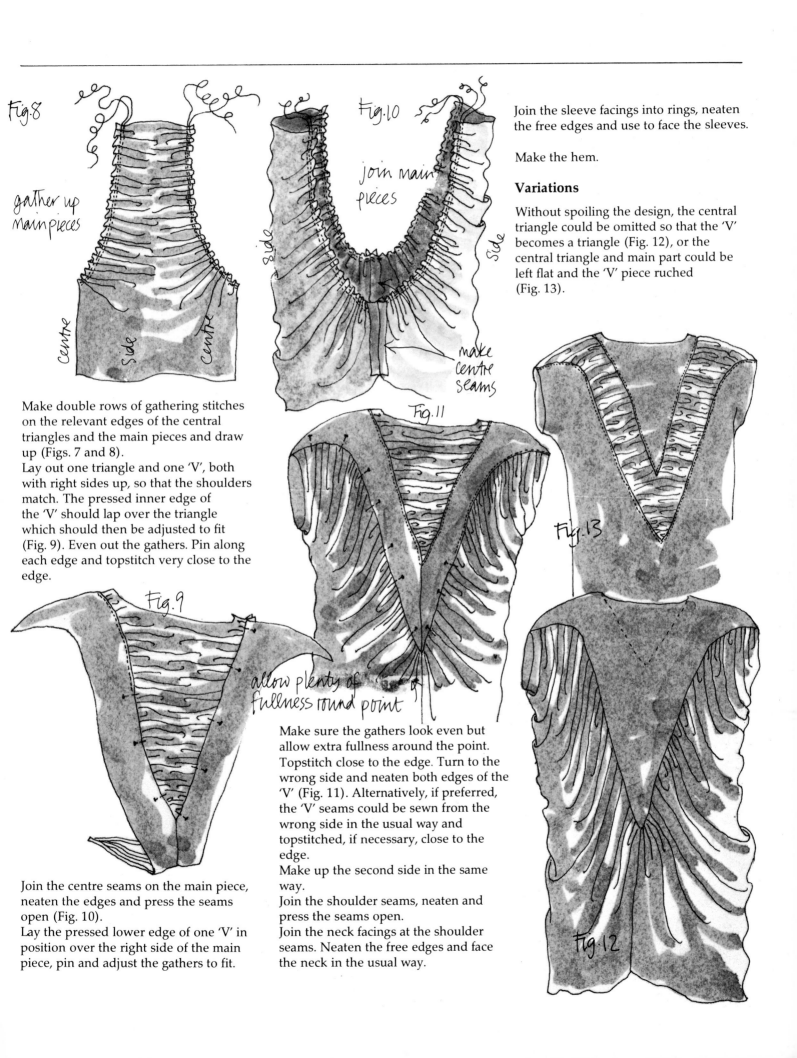

Fig. 8

gather up
main pieces

centre   side   centre

Fig. 10

side   join main pieces   side

make centre seams

Join the sleeve facings into rings, neaten the free edges and use to face the sleeves.

Make the hem.

Variations

Without spoiling the design, the central triangle could be omitted so that the 'V' becomes a triangle (Fig. 12), or the central triangle and main part could be left flat and the 'V' piece ruched (Fig. 13).

Make double rows of gathering stitches on the relevant edges of the central triangles and the main pieces and draw up (Figs. 7 and 8).
Lay out one triangle and one 'V', both with right sides up, so that the shoulders match. The pressed inner edge of the 'V' should lap over the triangle which should then be adjusted to fit (Fig. 9). Even out the gathers. Pin along each edge and topstitch very close to the edge.

Fig. 9

Fig. 11

allow plenty of fullness round point

Make sure the gathers look even but allow extra fullness around the point. Topstitch close to the edge. Turn to the wrong side and neaten both edges of the 'V' (Fig. 11). Alternatively, if preferred, the 'V' seams could be sewn from the wrong side in the usual way and topstitched, if necessary, close to the edge.
Make up the second side in the same way.
Join the shoulder seams, neaten and press the seams open.
Join the neck facings at the shoulder seams. Neaten the free edges and face the neck in the usual way.

Join the centre seams on the main piece, neaten the edges and press the seams open (Fig. 10).
Lay the pressed lower edge of one 'V' in position over the right side of the main piece, pin and adjust the gathers to fit.

Fig. 13

Fig. 12

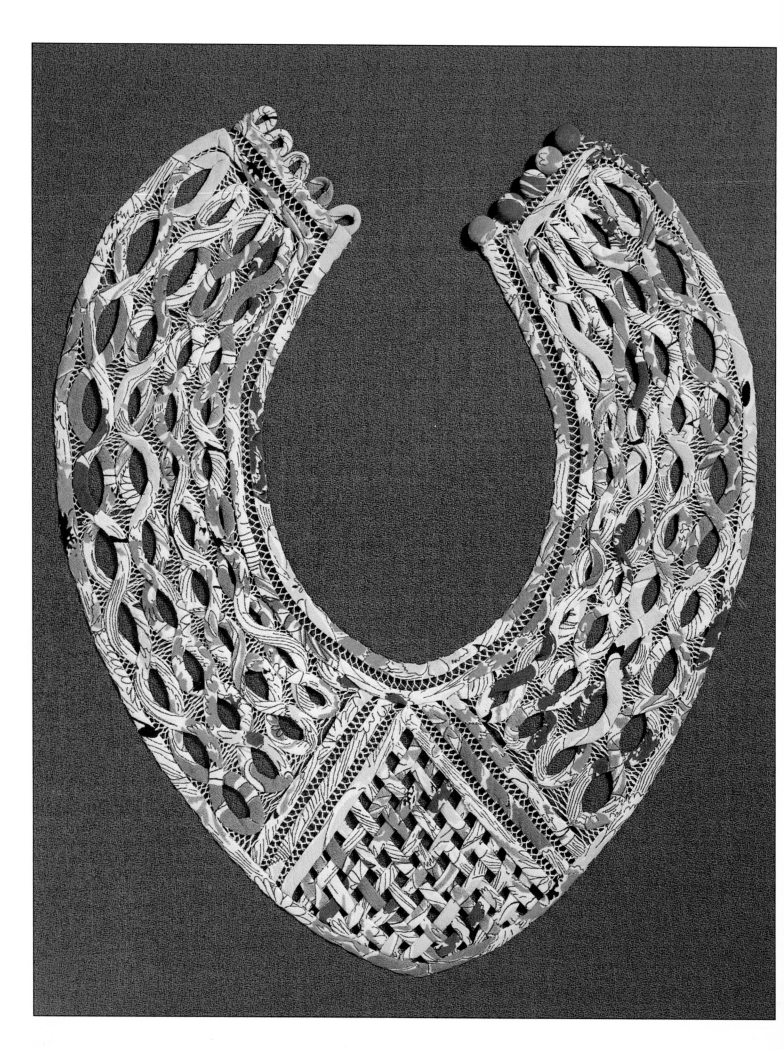

Faggoting

This somewhat curiously named technique is a way of joining pieces of fabric
to produce open decorative seams. There are many variations and it has endless uses.
At its most basic, it is a simple twisted stitch filling narrow gaps
between the sides of straight or slightly curved seams. At its most complex, a whole garment can be
made of rouleau strips faggoted together, creating a rich pattern and giving a most luxurious effect.
Some form of faggoting can be devised for use with almost all fabrics,
from the finest silk blouse crêpe to thick mohair coating. It is ideal for the embroiderer,
as the embroidery stitches which form the basis of the technique can be employed
to put a whole garment together, without the use of a sewing machine.
It also solves the problem of what to do with another piece of embroidery: wear it!
By varying the thickness of fabric and thread, but still using the same simple stitches,
faggoted clothes can look delicate and dainty, or simple and elegant.
Adapt it for use with any type of garment, from evening clothes to winter coats.

◄ This 1930s yoke was cut from its dress to be used as an accessory – what sacrilege!
It combines rouleau strips, made from a floral crêpe fabric, with 'simple faggoting' stitch,
a widely used method at that time.

Preparation

Faggoting is worked across a narrow gap between two pieces of fabric. To facilitate this, the two sides are tacked down onto a strip of paper.

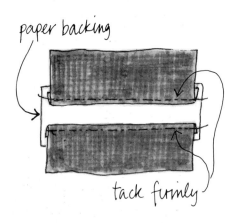

paper backing

tack firmly

● AVOID – using thick or stiff paper as this will make the work awkward to sew. The paper should be the lightest and softest that will hold the pieces of fabric apart. For instance, strong tissue paper will hold chiffon, voile, or crêpe de chine, but would not do for mohair (see the jacket project later in the chapter), which needs something stronger, such as a lightweight wrapping paper.

It is sometimes easier to use firm cotton fabric instead of paper, especially for large pieces of work .
Not only is it more pliable, but will not easily tear. The disadvantage is that the fabric will draw up more easily than would paper, making the faggoting uneven, so do use a rather stiff, paper-like material, that will neither stretch nor draw up easily.

Estimating the width of the gaps

The width of the gap between two pieces of fabric to be faggoted together must be worked out by experience. For the beginner, it is difficult to know where to start, so try this simple exercise: cut two strips of lightweight cotton measuring approximately 5in. by 2in., then press ½in. to the wrong side on one long edge of each strip (to neaten the edges of the seam). Firmly tack the neatened

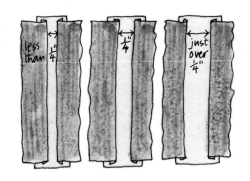

edges, centrally, to a light paper strip measuring 5in. by 2in., leaving a gap between them about ¼in. wide. Then make three, four or more similar strips, each one with the gap a slightly different width. Now look at the method for working 'simple faggoting stitch' and, using an ordinary well-twisted thread in the needle, link the strips together.

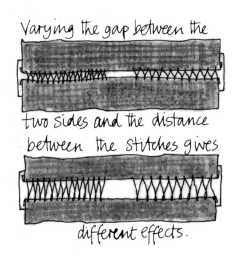

Varying the gap between the two sides and the distance between the stitches gives different effects.

● EXPERIMENT – with the various stitches using different widths of gaps until you are able to judge which is the most satisfactory. Note: when sewing the fabric to a paper backing for complete seams, you will soon find that you can use your eyes to judge the gaps, just as accurately and quickly as you did at the beginning with a tape measure.

The thread

The type and thickness of thread you use also affects the width of the gap. In

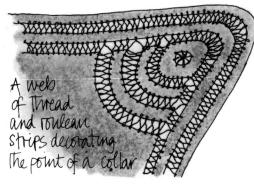

A web of thread and rouleau strips decorating the point of a collar

general, a thicker thread will work better on a wider gap than a thin one. However, though this might be effective on a sampler, which is static, it will probably not be so for clothes, where the hang, movement and general wear and tear will require something more substantial. Nevertheless, spiders' webs have their charms, and a spidery piece of faggoting may well make up in beauty what it loses in substance! At this point, it is important to stress that although faggoting may look delicate, it is actually quite strong, and even if accidently snagged it can usually be repaired. Anne Marie's jacket shown opposite is probably between 30 and 40 years old, while Miss J. Marton's blouse is even older, yet the stitches on both are still absolutely perfect. But back to the thread: usually one that is well twisted is the easiest to work with and therefore the best choice with which to start. Look at the pictures throughout this chapter. You will see that a wide variety of threads has been used, each giving a different effect. Such versatility, however, can only come with practice.

● EXPERIMENT – with many different types of thread for each of the many faggoting stitches to see how much variation can be devised.

● AVOID – using a thread so thick that it looks clumsy. Either widen the gap or sew each stitch a little further apart.

● AVOID – using too thin a thread so that it looks flimsy – narrow the gap or work the stitches closer together.

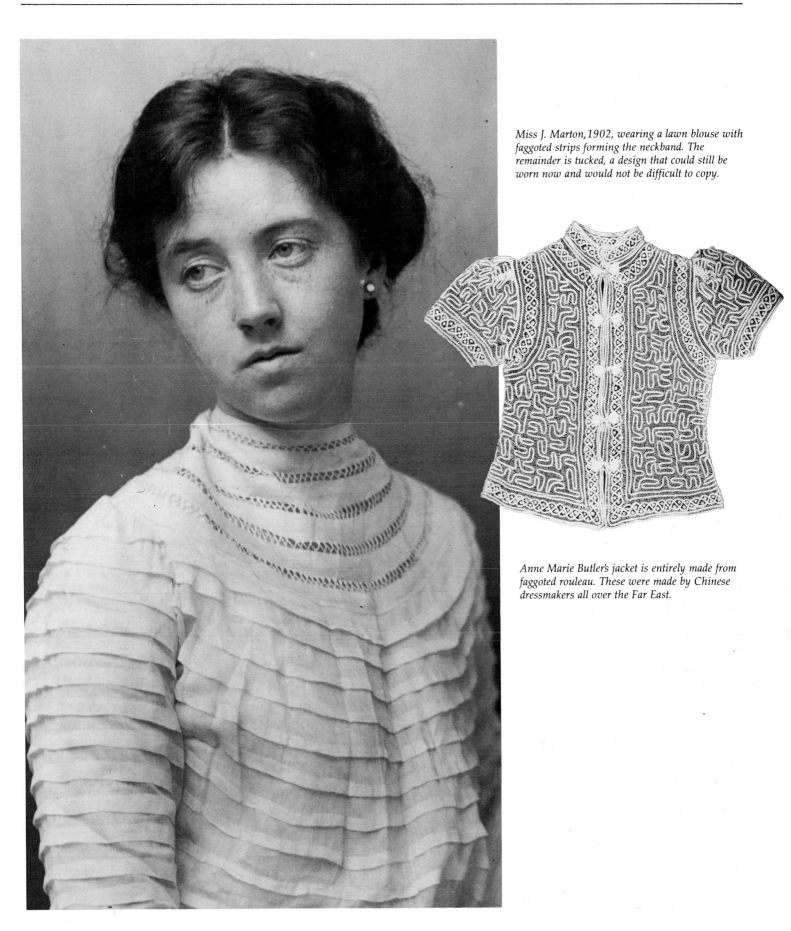

Miss J. Marton, 1902, wearing a lawn blouse with faggoted strips forming the neckband. The remainder is tucked, a design that could still be worn now and would not be difficult to copy.

Anne Marie Butler's jacket is entirely made from faggoted rouleau. These were made by Chinese dressmakers all over the Far East.

The stitches

There is much confusion between the names of all embroidery stitches, and nowhere more so than with the word 'faggoting'.

Here it is used to describe the technique, as do many books, but in some it is referred to under the general heading of 'insertion stitches', with faggoting being used to describe only a few of these. According to some sources, the name comes from a stitch used in drawn-thread work, where bundles of threads were tied together in groups forming 'faggots', a word which describes a bundle of twigs used for fuel.

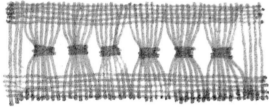

Try out the stitches that follow with different threads on different fabrics and so build up a group of samples you can use for reference.

● EXPERIMENT – with the spacing of the stitches. Work them close together or wider apart for different effects.

● AVOID – working the simpler stitches too far apart. The collar illustrated is sewn with approximately ten stitches to the inch.

● DO NOT WORRY – if fine stitches such as these are a little uneven. On most pieces they will be somewhere between eight and 12 stitches to every inch, which will not be apparent until you measure them.

Basic stitches

Three stitches are graced with the name 'faggoting': simple, twisted and knotted. These can be worked from either the right or wrong side. For ordinary seams it is often easier to work from the right side, but 'rouleau faggoting' (sampler, page 120) is almost always worked from the wrong side.

There are also innumerable other stitches with which to experiment.

1. Simple faggoting stitch

General notes: tack onto backing paper; can be worked from right to left or vice versa whichever is easiest; all stitches, except the first are worked with the needle inserted into the right side.

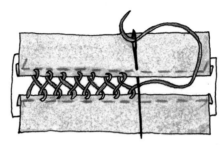

1. Bring the needle out on one side close to the end.
2. Bring the needle through on the second side a little to the right.
3. Hold the thread down with your left thumb and make the next stitch a little to the right on the opposite side, needle over thread.
Continue to end.

2. Twisted faggoting stitch

General notes: tack onto backing paper; work from left to right; insert the needle into the fabric on the underside and bring out onto the right side.

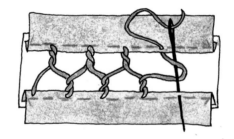

1. Bring the needle out close to the end.
2. Bring the needle through on the second side, a little to the right.
3. Put the needle *back* under the thread (i.e., right to left), twist the needle over the thread and insert for the next stitch a little to the right. Use your left thumb to hold each stitch as it is worked.
Continue to end.

3. Knotted faggoting stitch

General notes: tack onto backing paper; work from left to right; insert the needle on the right side and take it through to the wrong side.

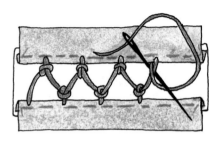

1. Bring the needle out on one side close to the end.
2. Bring it through on the second side slightly to the right forming a buttonhole stitch.
3. Take the needle back under the first buttonhole stitch, forming a second buttonhole stitch on top of the first. Repeat on other side slightly to the right and then continue to end.

Buttonhole faggoting

General notes: this can be done with or without tacking onto a paper or fabric backing depending on the fabric being used; work as for buttonhole stitch, turning the fabric round as each group of stitches are made; the groups can be varied in length and number of stitches and any variations of buttonhole stitch can be used.

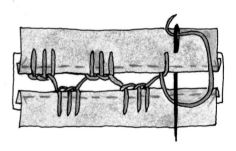

1. Make a group of buttonhole stitches on one side.
2. Turn the fabric and make another group on the other side.
Continue to end.

Woven faggoting

General notes: tack onto backing paper; all the stitches, except the first are stitched from front to back.
(Persistence pays; it is not really difficult, just complicated!)

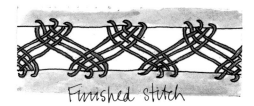

Finished stitch

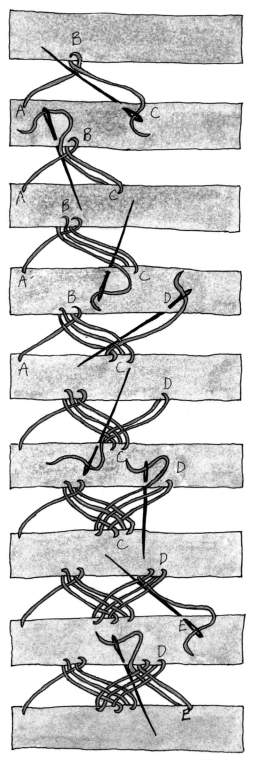

1. Bring needle out on right side at A. Make a stitch at B (needle over thread). Make a stitch at C (needle under thread between A and B).

2. Make a second stitch at B.

3. Make a second stitch at C, then weave needle over, under, over the three threads.

4. Make a stitch at D, then weave needle under, over, under the three threads.

5. Make a third stitch at C, then weave needle over, under, over the three threads.

6. Make a second stitch at D, then weave over, under, over the three threads.

7. Make a stitch at E, then weave needle under, over, under the three threads.

8. Make a third stitch at D, then weave needle over, under, over the three threads.
Repeat steps 3-8 and continue to end.

Bundled faggoting

General notes: tack onto backing paper; work from right to left; space the stitches widely apart or close together.
(Note that each complete stitch starts alternately at the top and bottom so that step 1 is worked in reverse for the second stitch and so on.)

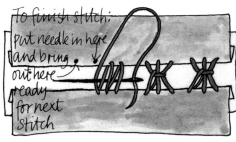

To finish stitch: put needle in here and bring out here ready for next stitch

1. Bring the needle out on the top edge, take straight down to lower edge and insert from the right side to the underside, then take it under the top edge a little to the left and bring it out on the surface of the fabric again.

2. Work another stitch in the same way.

3. Hold thread down with left thumb, take the needle back under these four threads and over held-down free thread. Bring needle through and pull up thread to form a 'bundle'. Complete by stitching into lower edge and coming up a little way along ready for the next stitch. Continue to end.

Antique seams

This is included because it is a quick and easy way to work a seam; it is not in the true sense 'faggoting'. It was often used to join selvedges together on simple embroidered linen garments made from rectangles of fabric,such as kaftans. It is usually worked without tacking onto a backing and from top to bottom. The stitches can be worked straight or slanting. Once you learn the knack of wrapping the cloth round two fingers and keeping the tension even on both, it is an easy and quick stitch to work.

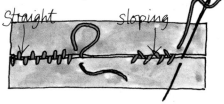

Straight   sloping

Suitable fabrics

As mentioned in the introduction to the chapter, nearly any fabric can be faggoted. Usually the technique is associated with the types of lightweight fabrics used for blouses, summer dresses, dressing gowns and underwear, and as much handwork is involved, it is sensible to use more expensive cloth to make the project worthwhile and so ensure items last as long as possible. Faggoting is especially successful with silk although faggoted seams can look beautiful on fine linens and cottons, particularly if the stitching is done with a silky thread.

Faggoted rouleau combined with pintucks

Blouses like this were an everyday sight from the 30s to the 50s. They were invariably worn with a 'costume' or suit and made from silk rayon or cotton, georgettes, voiles or muslins.

In general, a faggoting stitch can be found to use with most weights of fabric, but if the stitches are going to be used in conjunction with rouleau, the fabric must be suitable for cutting on the bias; it must also not fray too easily or the little tubes of fabric will soon fall apart at the seams.
(Turn to page 128 for details on making rouleau.)
Both plain and patterned fabrics can be used but patterns should obviously not be too dominant or the work will be hidden. Stripes and checks can

1930s silk georgette

1940s rays of faggoting on a rayon crêpe dress

Cotton dress – the stepped yoke seams are faggoted

sometimes be quite effective for faggoted rouleau if used carefully. A very wide or strongly coloured stripe would rarely work as it would look irregular, whereas a narrowly striped fabric in one or two colours might well be interesting.
Very stiff fabrics are sometimes faggoted together as the seams are then made more pliable – a conventional seaming would be too bulky.

Making faggoted clothes

To make a simple blouse or some other garment with faggoted seams, practise first on scraps and discover which stitches you like best. Soon you will be ready to decorate a garment, and if you can restrain yourself from making something composed entirely of faggoting, it might be more sensible to settle for a style similar to the ones

shown below. There are many simple loose-fitting blouse patterns available; one with fairly straight seams is ideal and you should be able to make it without altering the pattern and by cutting out the pieces in the normal way. To make it up, decide which seams you want to faggot rather than sew together. Neaten the edges and press the seam allowances to the wrong side. Tack the seams down onto paper (working a practice strip first to decide which stitch to use and the most suitable width of gap).
Work out the easiest order to make up the garment and then start with the smaller seams on collars and cuffs, yokes etc. In this way you can gradually build up the garment piece by piece.

● DO NOT – tack the whole garment together first. Work as described above.

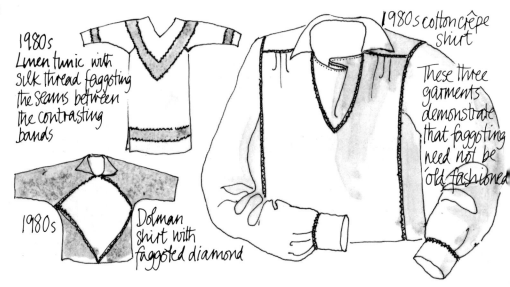

1980s Linen tunic with silk thread faggoting the seams between the contrasting bands

1980s Dolman shirt with faggoted diamond

1980s cotton crêpe shirt

These three garments demonstrate that faggoting need not be old fashioned

By German artist Ernst Dryden. Probably a design for a film, a dress with inset lines of faggoting.

Top: *A pleated dress, dated 1923, with an intricate faggoted bodice.*

Above: *Ethel Carhardt and Mrs Marton Saportas on the beach at Southampton, 1922. The dress on the left has horizontal groups of pintucks and a faggoted rouleau collar; the other has narrow bindings finishing the sleeves and petals around the neck.*

Faggoting with rouleau

The collar on page 127, the jacket on page 123 and the sampler are all made up using rouleau. Lengths of it are made up and then tacked in position on a ready drawn out design before being faggoted together working from the wrong side.

Making a rouleau motif:

Draw design on backing paper

Tack rouleau strips onto design

seam will show

Fill in with faggot stitch

wrong side

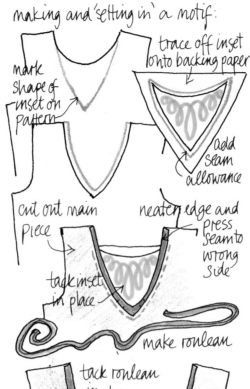

making and 'setting in' a motif:

mark shape of inset on pattern

trace off inset onto backing paper

add seam allowance

cut out main piece

neaten edge and press seam to wrong side

tack inset in place

make rouleau

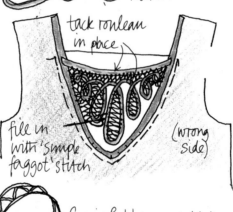

tack rouleau in place

fill in with 'simple faggot' stitch

(wrong side)

Easy substitutes for rouleau

To save time and work and still produce a similar effect, it is possible to substitute ready-made round braids for hand-made rouleau, and this can be worked in exactly the same way. There are also narrow ribbons available, as used by lacemakers, which can give attractive – but obviously different – results.

For the really fainthearted and lazy who cannot stand hand sewing and are about to give up on this technique, decorative work of a similar sort can be made using the method known as 'Indonesian faggoting', which involves no hand work at all. Once you have got the knack, it is easy to work out a whole range of designs, all of which are based on straight lines.

Start by cutting strips ¾in. wide. Press the edges over ¼in. to the wrong side and press in half.

Thin cotton strips   ¾"

neaten the edges

fold strip in half

For straight strips cut on straight grain. For curved strips cut on bias grain

these two bars are cut on the bias so that they will curve

Camisole, blouse and skirt made from 'Indonesian' faggoting

These could just as well be made using real faggoting!

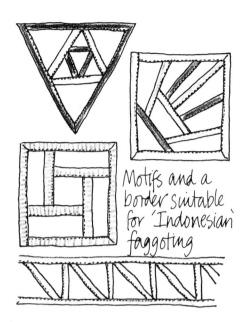

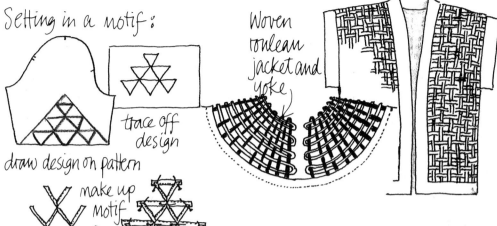

Setting in a motif:

trace off design

draw design on pattern

make up motif

Cut out sleeve, press seam to wrong side. Lay motif in place. Pin and stitch

Woven rouleau jacket and yoke

Motifs and a border suitable for 'Indonesian' faggoting

Draw a simple design for a motif or border and then work out how to make it up. For this example, start with the outer edge, bending the strip to form mitres at the corners and hold with pins.

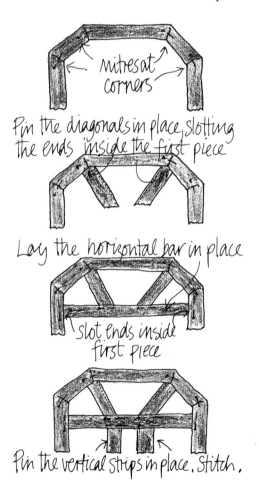

mitres at corners

Pin the diagonals in place, slotting the ends inside the first piece

Lay the horizontal bar in place

slot ends inside first piece

Pin the vertical strips in place. Stitch.

To use on a dress for example, mark the shape of the motif on the pattern, building up the design with several repeats of the motif as required. Add a seam allowance and cut away the inset. Make up the motifs and pin in place on each cut-out piece, a sleeve for instance. Stitch.

This technique can be used in many ways and in many places, as illustrated.

Woven rouleau

Another variation that avoids hand stitching involves weaving rouleau strips into motifs which are then used as insets.

Look at the yoke shown on page 120 ; the central diamond is made using this technique. The rouleau has been cut into lengths to fit, simply woven together to form a motif and then stitched in place firmly on the wrong side.

This variation can be used on any fabric suitable for making rouleau. A jacket made from a fine wool crêpe could be edged with woven rouleau, either in the same material or a contrast such as satin. Or try making cushion covers woven from different coloured pieces of rouleau on a contrasting background: an excellent way of using up remnants.

Modéle Jaquin, 1926. Oh dear, poor thing! But the decoration is terrific and not too difficult to copy. A version of 'Indonesian faggoting', but using rouleau.

This baggy jacket, unlike the other projects in the book, is cut from a diagram and needs no pattern. It was designed to encourage embroiderers or hand-stitchers with little or no dressmaking experience to 'have a go' at making clothes. Assembled entirely by hand, with no machine stitching at all, it consists of measured strips of fabric first neatened by hand and then faggoted together (Fig.1). For those of you used to sewing by hand it will prove very easy to make; to those dressmakers dedicated to their sewing machine it might seem rather daunting, but as the faggoting is done with extremely thick wool and large stitches it should present no problem. It is also surprisingly quick to complete (for example, the underarm and side seam took just 15 minutes to sew).

For those of you who prefer a neater look, simply leave off the revers, and if you do not want pockets, these too can be left out, thus simplifying the making up even further.

Fabric

For fabric, a very light, soft, brushed

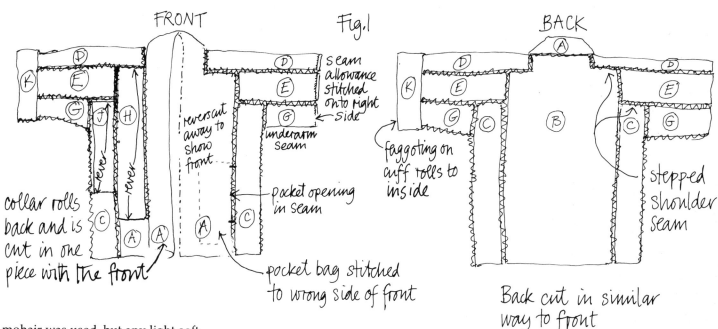

FRONT   Fig.1   BACK

seam allowance stitched onto right side

rever cut away to show front

underarm seam

pocket opening in seam

collar rolls back and is cut in one piece with the front

pocket bag stitched to wrong side of front

faggoting on cuff rolls to inside

stepped shoulder seam

Back cut in similar way to front

mohair was used, but any light soft material without a wrong or right side (both sides of the fabric show) will do. If you cannot find a double-sided material, instructions are given in Fig.3 for altering the pattern accordingly. This will result in the collar folding rather than rolling at the neck edge.

The wool used for the faggoting is an extremely thick knitting wool (similar to a rug wool but much softer), with the stitches about ¾in. apart. Two balls should be enough.

Size

The diagram (Fig.2) has been designed to fit sizes about 32in.–39in., with a finished back length of 30in. The sleeve length, from the nape of the neck to the wrist is approximately 30in. depending on how much the cuff is turned up.

Note: a 2in. hem has been included on the main jacket, ½in. seam allowances on all the other sides except cuffs, revers and collar which use the selvedge and therefore do not need stitching.

Cutting out

Referring to the cutting layout (Fig.3), cut out all the pieces to the measurements given. Mark each piece with a lettered paper tag, tacking it on firmly so that you do not become confused as to which piece is which.

Any discrepancy between the parts should be taken up by the width of the faggoting stitches.

Fig. 2

How to fit the pieces together:—

lower edge

18"

12½"

side seam

back

side back

side back

underarm

under sleeve

sleeve

under sleeve

underarm

side seam

side front

front and collar

pocket bag

side front

18"

12½"

cuff

selvedge

FOLD

centre back

back neck

selvedge

rever

rever

collar and front

lower edge

Front–Ⓐ is cut in one piece–shown opened out straight

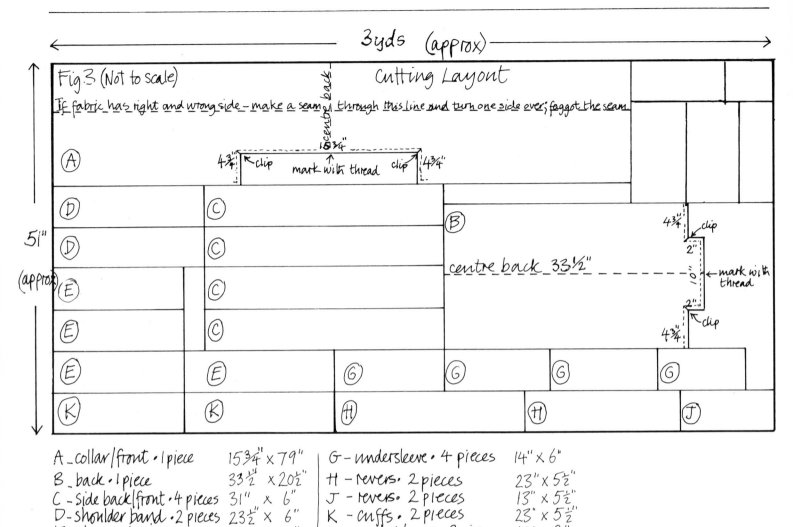

A – collar/front · 1 piece   15¾" x 79" | G – undersleeve · 4 pieces   14" x 6"
B – back · 1 piece   33½" x 20½" | H – revers · 2 pieces   23" x 5½"
C – side back/front · 4 pieces   31" x 6" | J – revers · 2 pieces   13" x 5½"
D – shoulder band · 2 pieces   23½" x 6" | K – cuffs · 2 pieces   23" x 5½"
E – sleeve · 4 pieces   20" x 6" | L – pocket bags · 2 pieces   13" x 9"

● REMEMBER – cut the cuffs, revers and collar along the selvedge as this is used as the finished edge.

● REMEMBER – if your fabric does not have a neat selvedge, you will need to add seam allowances on these edges.

● REMEMBER – mohair has a 'nap' or 'pile'. As you sew the pieces, arrange them so that the nap runs downwards, from the top to the bottom of the garment (i.e. from the neck to hem or wrist).

Preparation

To neaten the strips, begin by folding a seam allowance of ⅜in. onto the wrong side and oversew down to the main fabric using matching thread but do not let the stitches show on the right side. Do this on all the pieces, except the collar, cuffs, revers and pocket bags for which see notes below.

Collar (marked A) Turn ⅜in. seam allowances to the wrong side on the back neck, clipping into the corners (Fig.2); continue to lower edge.

Back (main piece marked B) Clip into the corners so that the seam allowances lie flat (Fig.3).

Sleeves (marked D, E and G) Turn the seam allowances on the lower ends on to the right side (i.e., the reverse way to the rest) and stitch as above.

Revers and cuffs (marked H, J and K) Fold seam allowances to the wrong side and stitch down firmly on one long side, (not the selvedge) and across both ends.

Pocket bags (marked as such) Stitch three sides as above, but with one of the long sides turned onto the right side and stitched in the same way.

Lay the jacket out with all the pieces in their correct position as shown in Fig.2.

To make up

It may not be necessary to tack the pieces onto backing paper, and with a little practise it should be easy to keep the two sides even. If it does prove difficult, however, tack the pieces onto paper before faggoting the pieces together, seam by seam, as described in the first part of this chapter. The stitch used is 'simple faggoting' (refer back to page 124).

Sleeves Remove pieces E and D from one sleeve and faggot them together. Start at the top and take great care not to stretch one side onto the other. Keep the stitches evenly spaced, about ⅝in. apart.

Remember that the top of E comes 3¾in. below the top of D (Fig.4).

Fig. 4

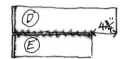

Next add the second strip marked E in the same way (Fig.5), then the two pieces marked G, again the tops of these starting 5in. below the top of E (Fig.6).

Lay the assembled sleeve back in position on the rest of the jacket and then make up the second sleeve in the same way. When complete, lay this back in place too.

Fig. 5

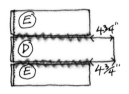

Fig. 6

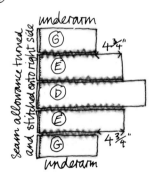

Back Faggot the two back pieces marked C in position on one side of B (Fig.7).
Pockets Faggot the pocket bag onto the remaining strips marked C as shown in Fig.8, from the top of the pocket down 7in.

Fig. 7

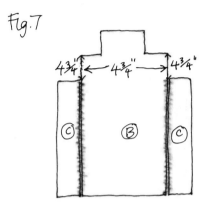

Fig. 8

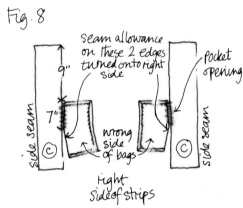

Fronts Faggot the pieces marked C onto A (Fig.9), stitching from the top to the faggoting on the pocket, and from the bottom of the faggoting on the pockets down to the hem.

Finish the pockets by laying the pocket bag in place on the wrong side of A, pin and then slip stitch in place (Fig.10).

● REMEMBER – to keep the tension of your stitches even so they are all the same size. It is only too easy to stitch them smaller and smaller or larger and larger.

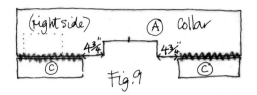

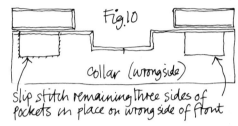

slip stitch remaining three sides of pockets in place on wrong side of front

Set the sleeves onto the back so that the top edge of the back comes halfway, about 2½in., across D (Fig.11).
Set the collar on the back and the sleeves Match the centre of the neck edge to the centre of the collar, setting the front corner of D into the corner of the 'cut out' on the collar, and fitting E and G in place as shown in Fig.12.

Fig. 11 Setting sleeves onto back

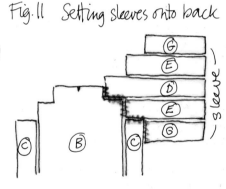

Fig. 12 Setting back and sleeves onto collar

Faggot across the top of G, up the side and across the top of E, up the side and half-way across the top of D, and then across the back neck, continuing up the other side and finishing across the top of G.

Underarms and side seams Fold the jacket in half through the shoulders, bringing the front and back edges of the sides and underarm seams together, and then faggot (Fig.13).

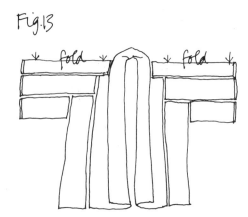

Fig.13

Set on cuffs Join the short edges of the cuffs together with faggoting (Fig.14). To set on the cuffs, make rows of gathering stitches across the lower end of the sleeves and draw up to fit the cuff (sleeve measures 24½in.; cuff, 20½in.).

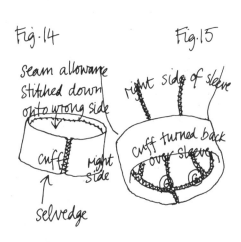

Fig.14   Fig.15

seam allowance stitched down onto wrong side

right side of sleeve

cuff   right side

cuff turned back over sleeve

selvedge

Wrap the cuff over the sleeve so that the hemmed edge butts up against the drawn-up end of the sleeve with seam in the cuff matching with the underarm seam on the sleeve (Fig.15). Faggot together firmly from the inside of the sleeve, i.e. from the wrong side as this seam shows slightly in wear.

Set on revers Position the piece marked J against H as shown in Fig.16. Faggot, then repeat for the other side. To set on the revers, position H against A so that the lower edge of H comes 7in. above the lower edge of A (Fig.17). Faggot in place.

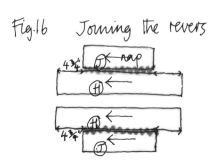

Fig.16   Joining the revers

Fig.17   Setting on the revers

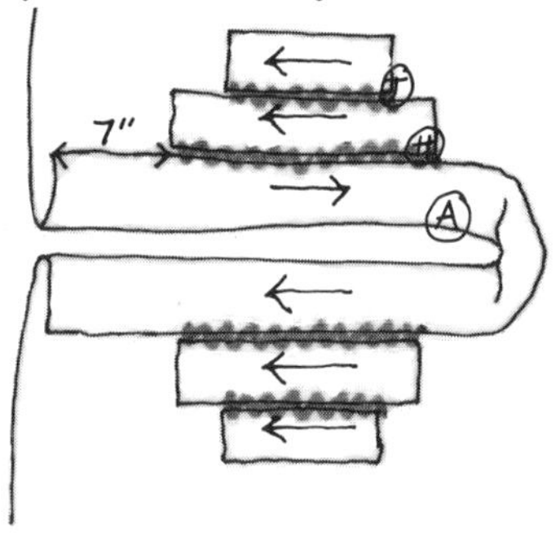

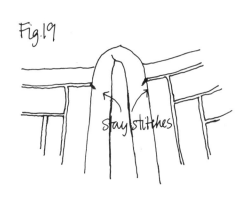

7"

Note: the nap on A goes up on one side and down on the other. If your fabric has a definite nap or pile, then cut A as two pieces. (Refer back to Fig.3.)

Hem Because the collar turns back, the hem has to be reversed at the front. Cut a step out of the front lower edge on each side of the front and turn hem up as shown (Fig.18).

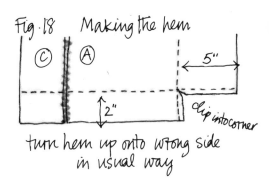

Fig.18   Making the hem

C   A   5"

2"   clip into corner

turn hem up onto wrong side in usual way

Fig.19

stay stitches

Finishing With the jacket thus completed, press from the wrong side and finally, if required, work a small stay stitch where indicated in Fig.19 to help the collar to hang properly.

General Notes

The information that follows is relevant to all the techniques and projects described in this book. Read it carefully before starting to work on the projects.

Finding and choosing fabrics

I prefer to look for fabrics in the exuberant shops found in, or near to, markets and rag trade areas, rather than in the more decorous departments in large stores.

These small shops often stock an enormous variety, ranging from cheap cottons to the best silks and woollens, plus a good measure of the unusual materials used for the more outrageous fashions, bought in from clothes manufacturers' end-of-season remnants, and so reflecting the new ideas and fashion trends.

Department stores are generally not as interested in unusual fabrics, and may not be as quick to stock them. However, as they do have a vast array of different types, something interesting can often be found. Most are reliable for such basic fabrics as tweeds, wool, crêpe, lawn and poplin, usually in a range of several colours.

Dressmakers usually understand that when buying a fabric, they must be guided by some reference to the use to which it will be put – coat, blouse, dress, or whatever; in other words, the weight and 'handle' or feel of fabric required. Some qualify this further, especially with wool, 'tweed', 'crêpe', flannel . . . (i.e. the weave). But I find that many of my students are unaware that the same applies to other fibres, such as cotton, linen and silk, together with most of the synthetics. Thus silk and cotton can be woven into 'tweed' or 'crêpe' or knitted up into 'jersey' just as much as the better known fabrics usually made from these fibres, such as satin and chiffon or poplin and lawn.

Here are some guidelines to follow when buying fabric:

● DO NOT – confuse fibre and weave. Silk, rayon, polyester nylon and cotton are fibres; satin, twill, crêpe, velvet and taffeta are the names of weaves. Jersey is a knitted fabric.

● DO NOT – confuse price with quality. Beautifully made and designed silks generally from the Far East, are often much cheaper than mundane cottons, even when from the same shop. Fashion affects price too: linen has become much more expensive since it recently became fashionable, especially in the larger stores. So if you like it, buy it, even if it seems very cheap!

● BEFORE – choosing a fabric to use with any of the techniques in the book, read the notes in the relevant chapter.

● AVOID – buying fabric in a hurry. Take time! Shop around! Examine clothes similar to those you want to make to see what sort of fabric has been used – how thick or thin, how soft or stiff etc.

● ALWAYS – take a tape measure with you, and the layout of the pattern you intend to use. If you are working with our patterns, for example, take notes of the sizes –lengths and widths – of individual pieces of a garment: e.g. *front blouse – 22in. × 14in. wide approximately (without facing) long sleeve – 22in. × 16in. wide.*

This will make it much easier to work out exactly how much, or little, you need – especially important when you find the perfect fabric is a remnant or extremely expensive!

● ALWAYS – hold the fabric up against you and look in a mirror to see how it hangs, how it feels, how the pattern or print looks when broken up.

Cutting out

Before cutting into any fabric it is a good idea to shrink it by washing; this also applies to any interlining.

I prefer to mark around a pattern with chalk (sometimes with pencil), rather than pinning the pattern to the fabric, and then cutting through the chalk line. This method has two advantages: it is more accurate and makes it much easier to re-arrange the layout, especially when using commercial paper patterns which only have one piece for the sleeve, half a front and so on.

Use weights to hold the pattern in place on the fabric and a tape measure to check that the grainline is parallel to the selvedge.

Next, use well-sharpened tailors' chalk (flat pieces) to mark around the pattern. Cut out using large shears; do not 'nibble' the fabric but use the full length of the blades so that the pieces have neat, straight edges. Jagged edges lead to inaccuracy.

Check small pieces against the pattern to ensure they are absolutely accurate. Where notches are shown, mark with chalk and then clip about ⅛in. into the edge; also mark the centre front and back with notches.

Interlining (or interfacing)

This is a vexed question these days. When I started work for a high class manufacturer, in the 1950s, everything was interlined – every facing, pocket, tab, band and belt. This involved lots of work but was fine for the structured look of the times.

Nowadays, except on the most expensive clothes, interlining is almost entirely restricted to restraining very stretchy edges, mostly on jersey fabric. This is not only because of the extra expense involved, but also because recent fashion has a softer and less structured look, and interlining would detract from this.

There are three reasons for using interlining:

a) to stop stretching

b) to prevent the impression of a seam edge showing on the right side after pressing

c) to give body, to stiffen, or to strengthen an edge. (The last of these applies particularly where buttons and buttonholes are used.)

Nothing marks clothes out as being 'homemade' more often than inappropriate interlining. The non-woven fabric especially made for the purpose, is one of the main culprits – it is more like paper than fabric and thus imparts a paper-like quality to any garment made with it – fine if you want to dress in paper clothes, but not otherwise!

Inexperienced dressmakers also tend to use interlinings that are too thick and stiff, producing a clumsy effect. If it *is* necessary to interline something, it is most important to use the correct weight of interlining for that fabric. Usually I use lawn as it is thin and soft – though the more structured look, now creeping over the horizon, means that I am beginning to use slightly firmer cottons. Another trap for the inexperienced to fall into is knowing where exactly to put the interlining. Commercial paper patterns are often sloppy about this, which only adds to the confusion. If the interlining is to be used to stop impressions showing through on the right side, it is important to understand that it must be attached to the wrong side of the main fabric *not* the wrong side of the facing, so that it lies between the main fabric and the seam allowance and therefore acts as a buffer when pressed. It will still fulfil the other purposes for which it is used.

Adapting patterns

A few pieces of equipment are needed especially for this. These are:

a) a tracing wheel (this should have needle-sharp metal points sticking out all round; some of the plastic ones are not sharp and therefore useless)

b) a yardstick (or metric equivalent) and ruler

c) a large set square (often useful but not essential)

d) paper – special paper, each piece 1yd. square, printed in inch squares and sub-divided into ½in. squares, is the easiest to use. Alternatively any large sheets of paper will do, but will involve more work on your part.

Specific instructions are given in each chapter for adapting a suitable commercial pattern for the project. However some general advice may be helpful.

Reference lines Use these in conjunction with a yardstick to align the pieces of a pattern that has been cut up and spread out to allow extra fabric for pleats, pintucks etc.

Tracing off This can be done with tracing paper in the usual way, or more practically, on a large scale, with a tracing wheel. Lay the part that is to be 'traced off' on a piece of pattern paper placed over a thick pad of paper (newspaper would be fine) to ensure the impressions show through. Run the tracing wheel firmly along the required lines; an impression should show up clearly on the new paper.

Remember when tracing off two adjacent pieces to move the pattern over to allow enough space for the seam allowances to be added to each side of the new seam.

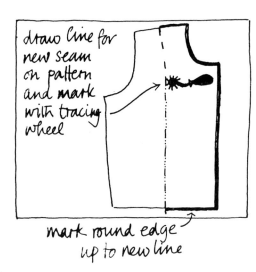

draw line for new seam on pattern and mark with tracing wheel

mark round edge up to new line

move pattern over

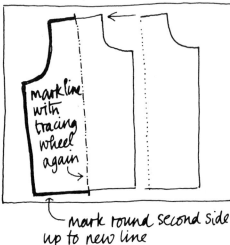

mark line with tracing wheel again

mark round second side up to new line

add seam allowance to both sides cut out

Seams Make these anywhere they are needed using the above method; they need not always be straight, but can be curved or angled.

Making up

Before starting to make up a garment, do read the instructions and follow them in the order given. Each seam must be pressed thoroughly and the edges finished (or neatened) where necessary *before* sewing across it. To neglect this is another way to achieve the 'homemade' look!

Toiles (or roughs)

Making up a rough of a garment, called a toile, is necessary where major alterations have been made to a pattern; this is to show how the new version will fit as well as how it will look. If you are reasonably experienced, they are not necessary for small adjustments. Use cheap cotton or old sheets, and make up exactly as the finished garment apart from facings and finishing off seams. A toile may need altering several times before it is perfect; then take it apart and use the corrected individual pieces as your pattern, or copy the alteration onto the original paper pattern.

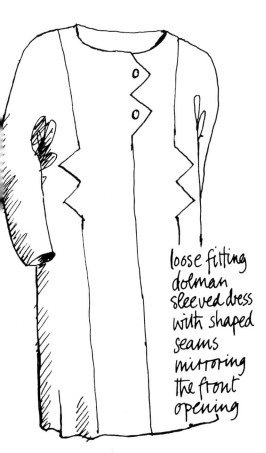

loose fitting dolman sleeved dress with shaped seams mirroring the front opening

Drawing by Ernst Dryden, 1930s. The suit on the left illustrates the use of seams as decoration – note the clever way the neck and lower edge of the blouse echo the shaped seams.

More on pleats and tucks

Pleats and tucks cover such a wide spectrum that I ran out of space in the chapter, so I am adding two more examples of adaptations that can be made here.

The first example shows how easy it is to allow for pleats and tucks on an existing pattern.
Take a basic pattern like this:

The second example illustrates one way of shaping the ends of pleats fit when the edge of the piece is curved.
Take a basic pattern like this:

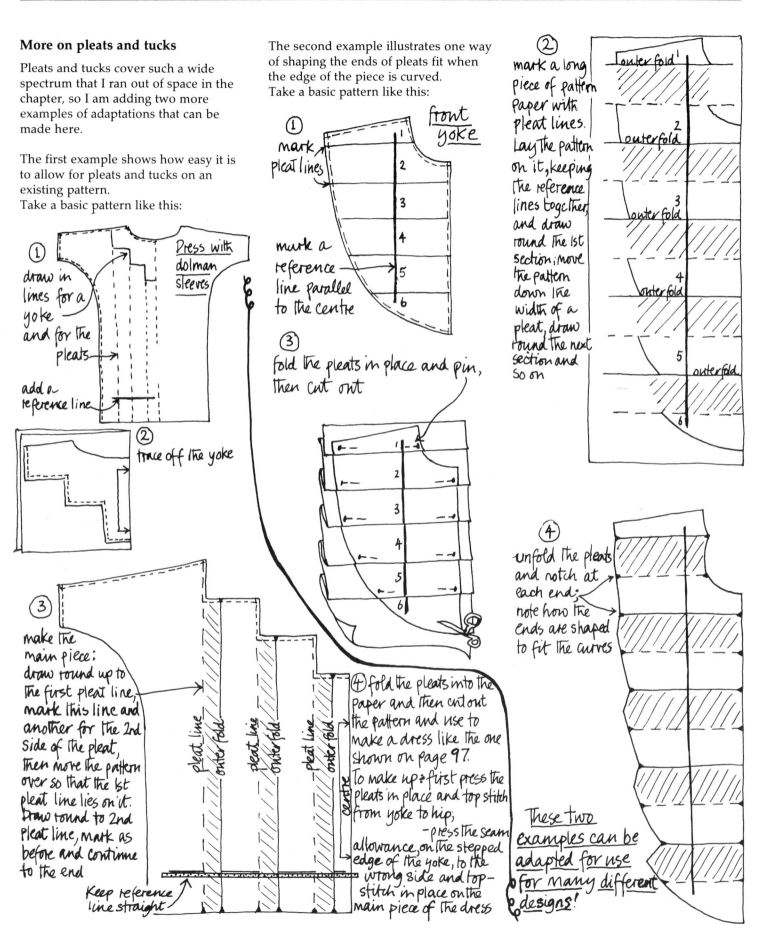

① draw in lines for a yoke and for the pleats→

add a reference line

Dress with dolman sleeves

② trace off the yoke

③ make the main piece: draw round up to the first pleat line, mark this line and another for the 2nd side of the pleat, then move the pattern over so that the 1st pleat line lies on it. Draw round to 2nd pleat line, mark as before and continue to the end

Keep reference line straight

① mark pleat lines

front yoke

mark a reference line parallel to the centre

③ fold the pleats in place and pin, then cut out

④ fold the pleats into the paper and then cut out the pattern and use to make a dress like the one shown on page 97.
To make up: first press the pleats in place and top stitch from yoke to hip;
— press the seam allowance, on the stepped edge of the yoke, to the wrong side and top-stitch in place on the main piece of the dress

② mark a long piece of pattern paper with pleat lines. Lay the pattern on it, keeping the reference lines together, and draw round the 1st section; move the pattern down the width of a pleat, draw round the next section and so on

outer fold
outer fold
outer fold
outer fold
outer fold

④ unfold the pleats and notch at each end; note how the ends are shaped to fit the curves

These two examples can be adapted for use for many different designs!

138

Pattern Diagrams

The patterns that follow on pages 140–151 are for nine of the projects in the book. The instructions in each chapter for adapting commercial paper patterns will not be needed if you use these patterns. *But* the making up (sewing) instructions for each chapter apply to both my patterns and adapted commercial patterns. If you decide to work from *my* patterns there are several points to remember.

Sizes

These are based on:

	Small	Medium	Large
Bust	34–36in.	36–38in.	38–40in.
Hips	36–38cm	38–40in.	40–42in.

In most cases, the diagrams are drawn up to fit 'medium', and 'large'.
All the clothes, with the exception of the striped dress on page 32 and the flounced dress on page 19, are designed to be very loose fitting, and are therefore suitable for quite a wide range of sizes.

Waist measurement This is not included as it is not applicable to most of the designs in the book but where it is, it is easy to alter by making larger or smaller tucks.

Length Most of the designs are suitable for a height of approximately 5ft. 6in., but lengths vary according to the style. For instance, the flounced dress is cut to just below the knee, whereas the bound coat on page 93 is much longer.

● BEWARE – most of the clothes are designed to be very loose so do think before you make them much shorter as this *may* spoil the proportion.

Seam allowances of ⅝in. are included, except where specified on the diagram. But the dotted lines, (indicating pocket outlines, patch pockets or bands,) on a pattern piece, do *not* include seam allowances; in these cases they must be added.
Squares on the diagrams each represent a 2in. square.

Symbols ◄——► indicates the straight grain and should be laid parallel to the selvedges;
↓———↓ indicates the edge pointed to, the centre of the piece, and *not* a cut edge. Such edges should be laid against a fold on the straight grain of the fabric. In both cases the grain is usually taken to be parallel to the selvedge, but can just as well be used at right angles to it.

Pattern paper, printed in inch squares, provides the easiest way to scale up the patterns.
Drawing up a diagram *Before* cutting out the pieces, check that all relevant pieces match, e.g. both edges of the side or shoulder seams, sleevehead to armhole (remember to allow for any ease or tucks on the sleevehead), collar to neck, notches for pocket openings on a seam to those on the pocket.
On small pieces, or tight curves, it is quicker and more accurate to do this by marking and measuring the stitching line; measuring the edge of a curved seam is *not* accurate.

● NOTE – it is easier, when laying the pattern on the fabric, if pieces cut to the fold are cut from folded paper, i.e. both sides of a piece rather than one half.

● DO – write on each pattern piece all relevant information: the name of the garment; the name of the part; any special information or instructions; the date used; details of fabric together with the amount and width used.

Finally, mark the pattern, or alter it, to match any alterations made to the garment, thus making subsequent use quicker and easier.

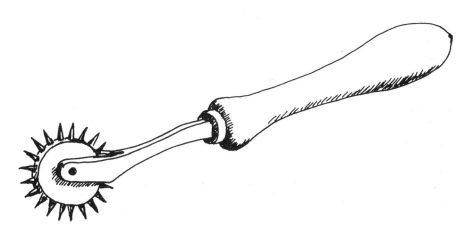

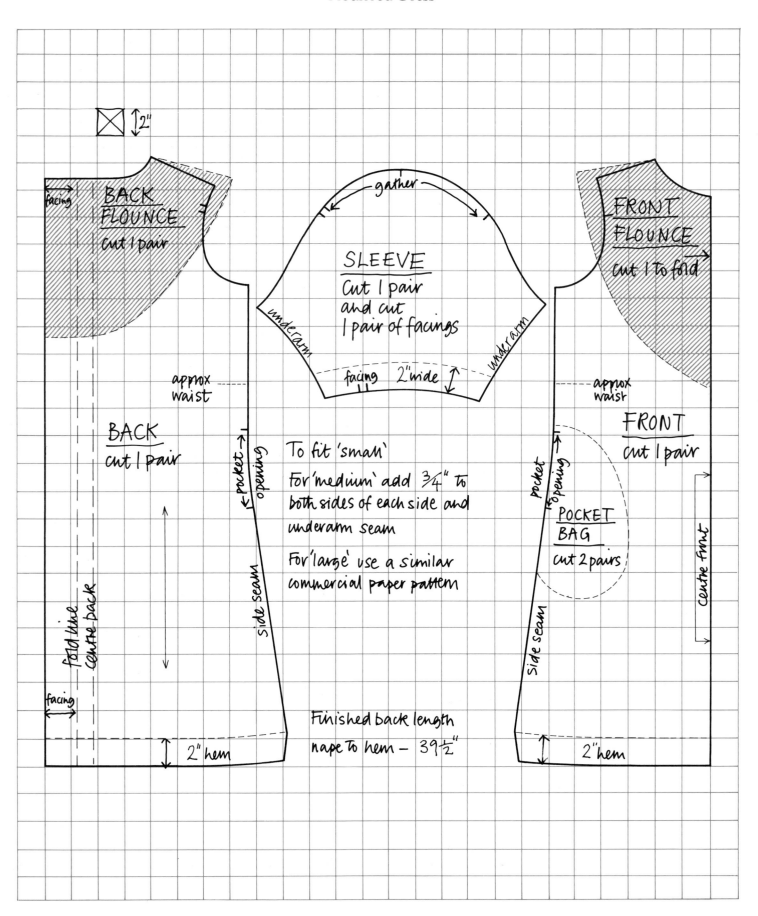

2"

BACK
FLOUNCE
cut 1 pair

facing

SLEEVE
Cut 1 pair
and cut
1 pair of facings

gather

underarm

underarm

facing   2" wide

FRONT
FLOUNCE
cut 1 to fold

approx
waist

approx
waist

BACK
cut 1 pair

pocket opening

side seam

fold line centre back

facing

FRONT
cut 1 pair

pocket opening

POCKET
BAG
cut 2 pairs

side seam

centre front

To fit 'small'

For 'medium' add ¾" to
both sides of each side and
underarm seam

For 'large' use a similar
commercial paper pattern

Finished back length
nape to hem – 39½"

2" hem

2" hem

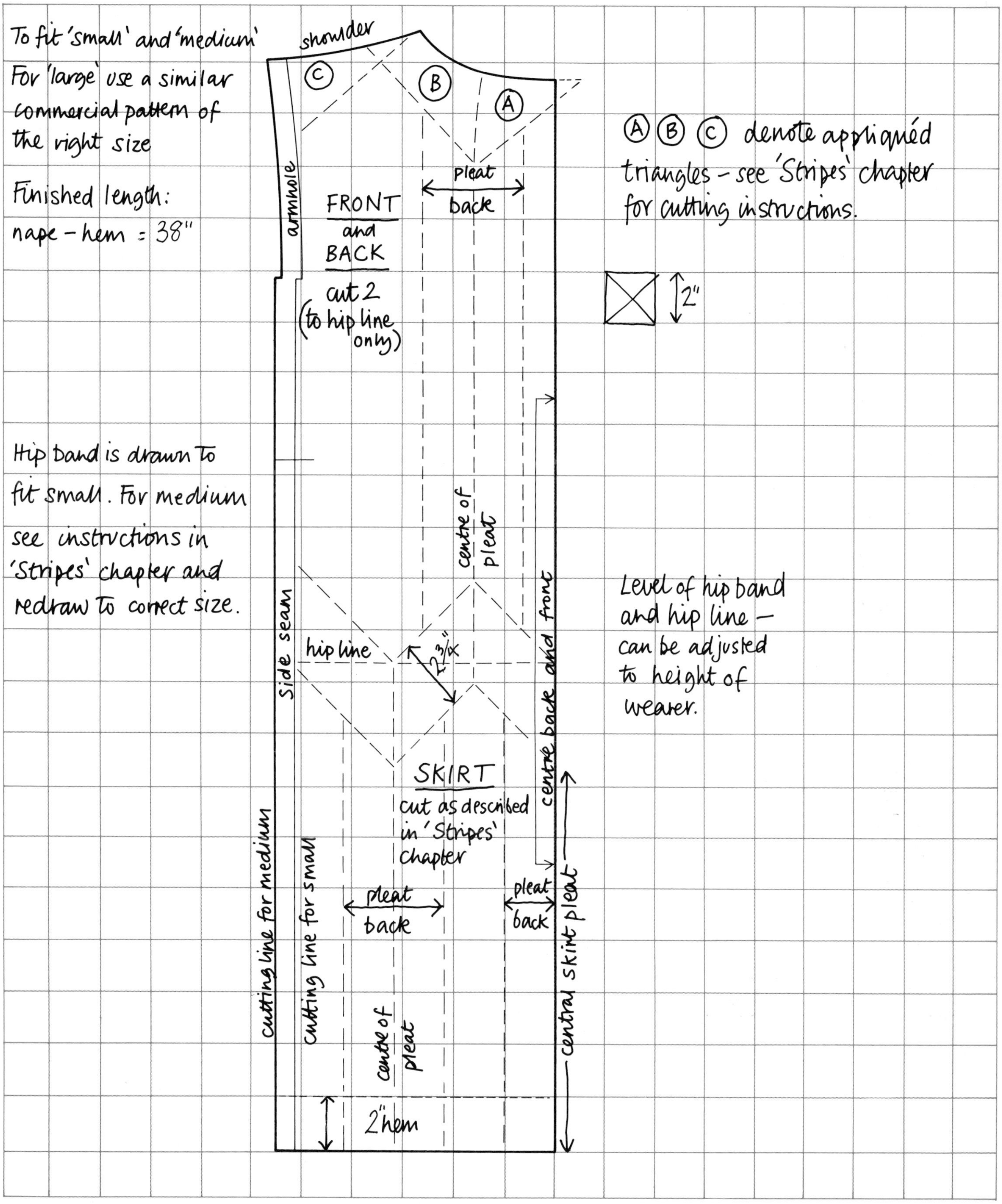

To fit 'small' and 'medium'
For 'large' use a similar
commercial pattern of
the right size

Finished length:
nape − hem = 38"

shoulder

Ⓒ   Ⓑ   Ⓐ

armhole

pleat
back

FRONT
and
BACK

cut 2
(to hip line
only)

Ⓐ Ⓑ Ⓒ denote appliquéd
triangles − see 'Stripes' chapter
for cutting instructions.

⊠ ↕ 2"

Hip band is drawn to
fit small. For medium
see instructions in
'Stripes' chapter and
redraw to correct size.

centre of
pleat

side seam

hip line   ↖ 3/x ↘

Level of hip band
and hip line −
can be adjusted
to height of
wearer.

centre back and front

SKIRT

cut as described
in 'Stripes'
chapter

pleat
back

pleat
back

central skirt pleat

cutting line for medium

cutting line for small

centre of
pleat

↕ 2" hem

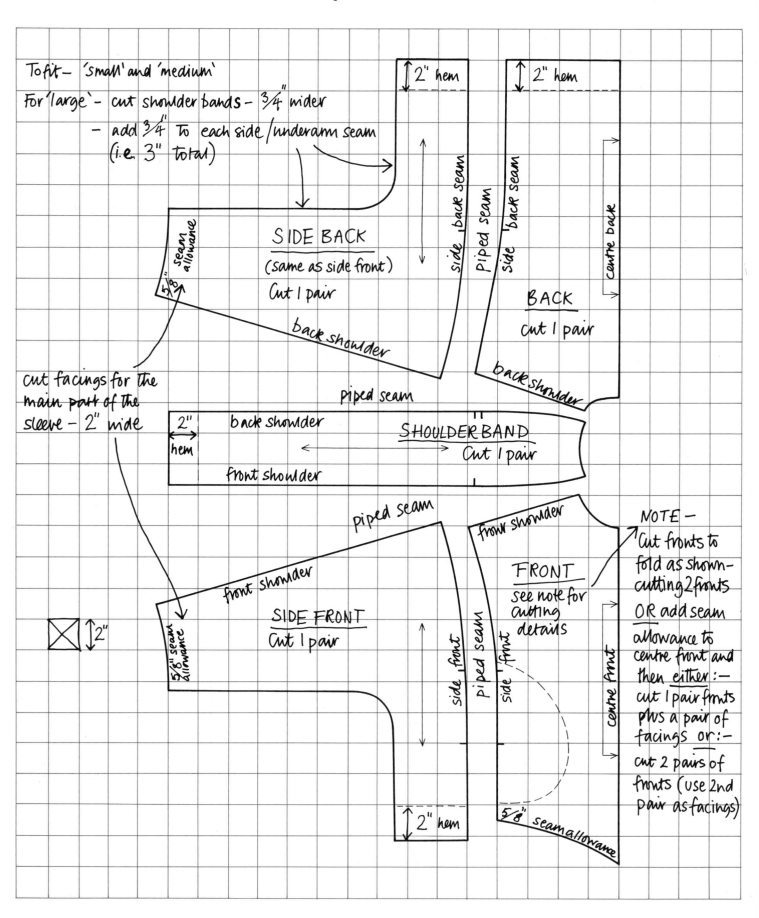

To fit – 'small' and 'medium'

For 'large' – cut shoulder bands – ¾" wider
  – add ¾" to each side / underarm seam
    (i.e. 3" total)

5/8" seam allowance

SIDE BACK

(same as side front)

Cut 1 pair

back shoulder

cut facings for the main part of the sleeve – 2" wide

2" hem

side back seam

Piped seam

side back seam

centre back

BACK

cut 1 pair

back shoulder

piped seam

2" hem

back shoulder

SHOULDER BAND

Cut 1 pair

front shoulder

Piped seam

front shoulder

front shoulder

front shoulder

2"

5/8" seam allowance

SIDE FRONT
Cut 1 pair

side front

Piped seam

side front

FRONT

see note for cutting details

centre front

NOTE –

Cut fronts to fold as shown – cutting 2 fronts OR add seam allowance to centre front and then either :–
cut 1 pair fronts plus a pair of facings or :–
cut 2 pairs of fronts (use 2nd pair as facings)

2" hem

5/8" seam allowance

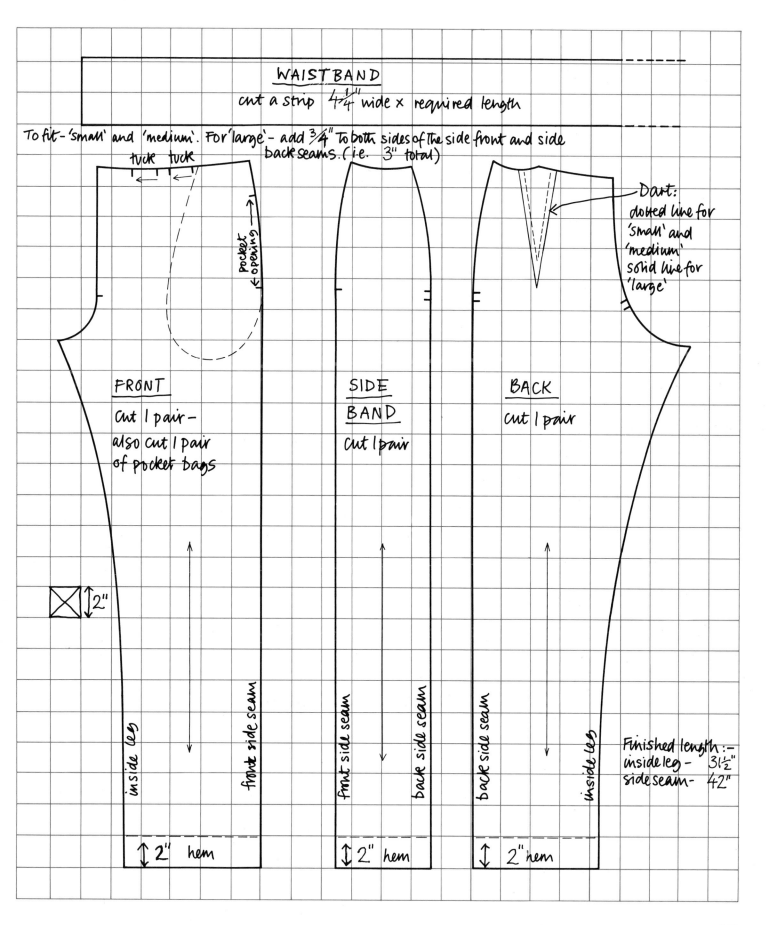

WAISTBAND

cut a strip $4\frac{1}{4}"$ wide x required length

To fit - 'small' and 'medium'. For 'large' - add ¾" to both sides of the side front and side back seams. (i.e. 3" total)

tuck tuck

pocket opening

Dart:
dotted line for
'small' and
'medium'
solid line for
'large'

FRONT

Cut 1 pair -
also cut 1 pair
of pocket bags

SIDE
BAND

Cut 1 pair

BACK

cut 1 pair

⊠ ↕2"

inside leg

front side seam

front side seam

back side seam

back side seam

inside leg

↕2" hem

↕2" hem

↕ 2" hem

Finished length :-
inside leg - 31½"
side seam - 42"

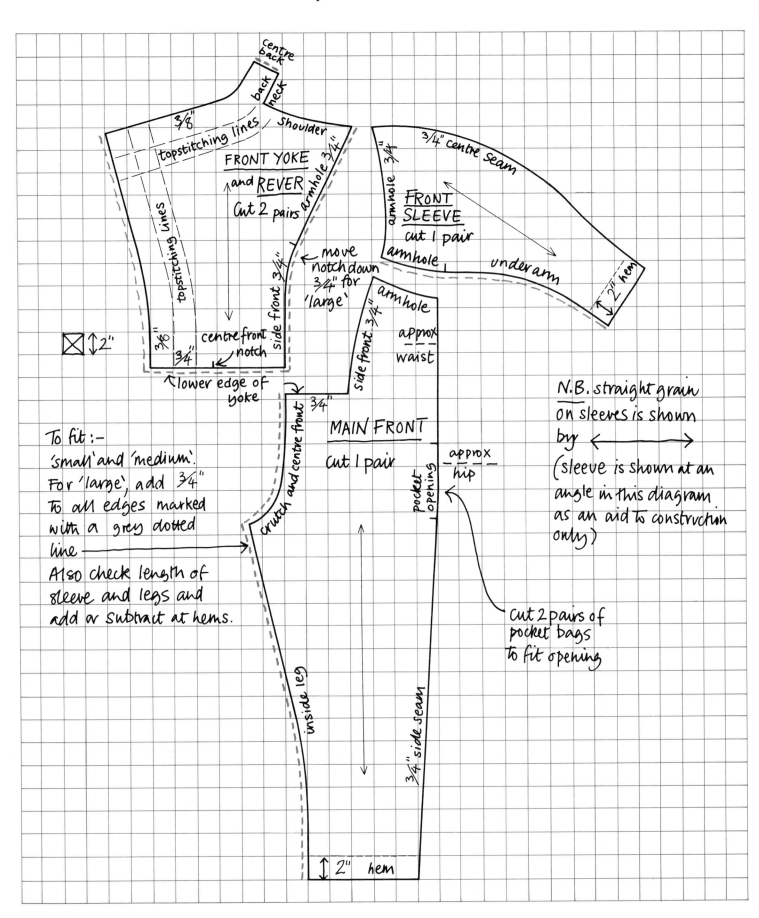

centre back

back neck

3/8"
topstitching lines / shoulder

FRONT YOKE
and REVER
Cut 2 pairs

armhole 3/4"

topstitching lines

3/8"

3/4"

centre front notch

side front 3/4"

↑ lower edge of yoke

move notch down 3/4" for 'large'

3/4" centre seam

armhole 3/4"

FRONT SLEEVE
cut 1 pair

armhole

underarm

2" hem

⊠ ↕2"

armhole 3/4"

side front 3/4"

approx waist

To fit :—
'small' and 'medium'.
For 'large', add 3/4"
To all edges marked
with a grey dotted
line ————————→
Also check length of
sleeve and legs and
add or subtract at hems.

crutch and centre front

3/4"

MAIN FRONT
Cut 1 pair

pocket opening

approx hip

N.B. straight grain
on sleeves is shown
by ⟵——————⟶
(sleeve is shown at an
angle in this diagram
as an aid to construction
only)

cut 2 pairs of
pocket bags
to fit opening

inside leg

3/4" side seam

↕2" hem

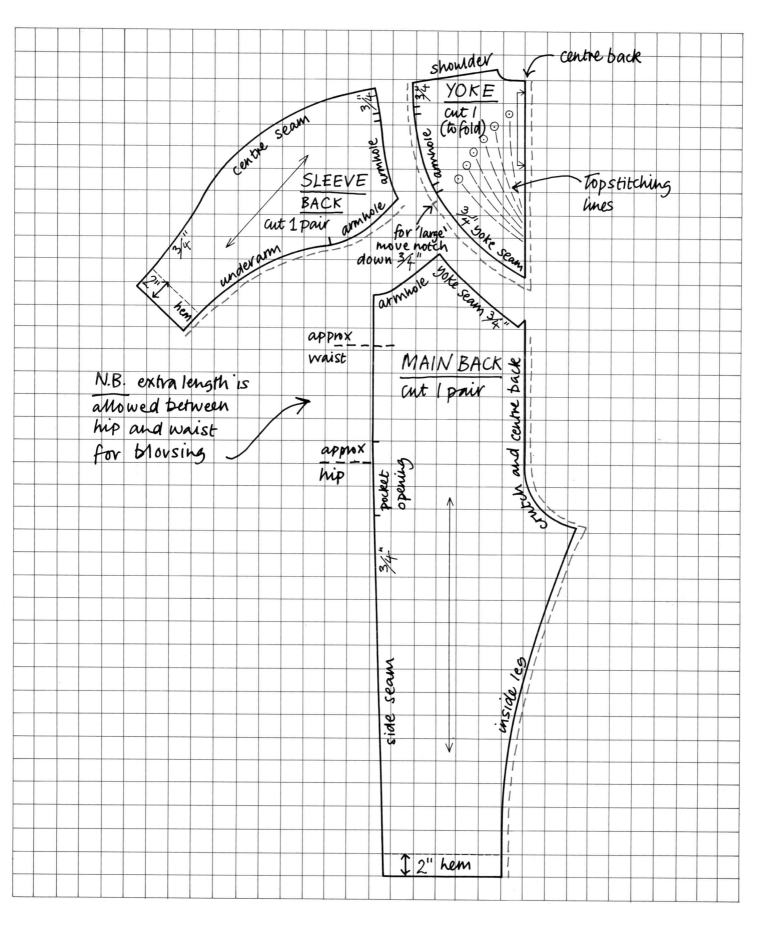

centre back

shoulder

YOKE
cut 1
(to fold)

3/4

Topstitching lines

centre seam

3/4"

SLEEVE
BACK
cut 1 pair

armhole

armhole

armhole

3/4" yoke seam

3/4"

underarm

2"

hem

for 'large' move notch down 3/4"

armhole

yoke seam 3/4"

approx
waist

MAIN BACK
cut 1 pair

N.B. extra length is allowed between hip and waist for blousing

approx
hip

crotch and centre back

pocket opening

3/4"

side seam

inside leg

2" hem

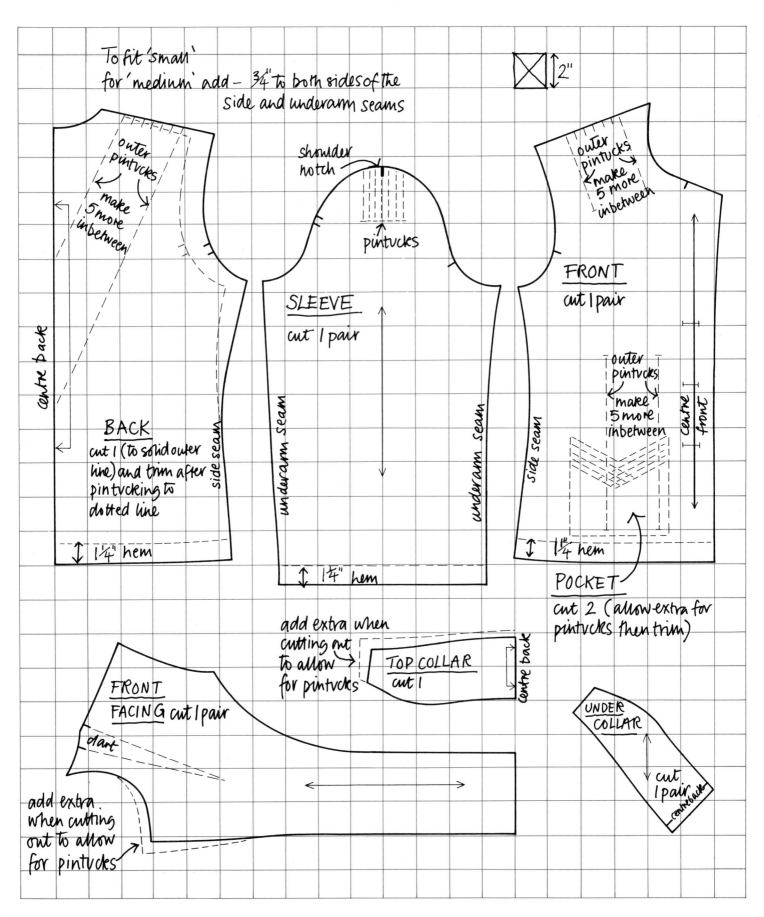

To fit 'small'
for 'medium' add – ¾" to both sides of the
side and underarm seams

2"

outer pintucks
make 5 more inbetween

shoulder notch

pintucks

outer pintucks
make 5 more inbetween

FRONT
cut 1 pair

SLEEVE
cut 1 pair

centre back

BACK
cut 1 (to solid outer line) and trim after pintucking to dotted line

side seam

underarm seam

underarm seam

side seam

outer pintucks
make 5 more inbetween

centre front

1¼" hem

1¼" hem

1¼" hem

POCKET
cut 2 (allow extra for pintucks then trim)

add extra when cutting out to allow for pintucks

TOP COLLAR
cut 1

centre back

FRONT
FACING cut 1 pair

dart

UNDER COLLAR

cut 1 pair

centre back

add extra when cutting out to allow for pintucks

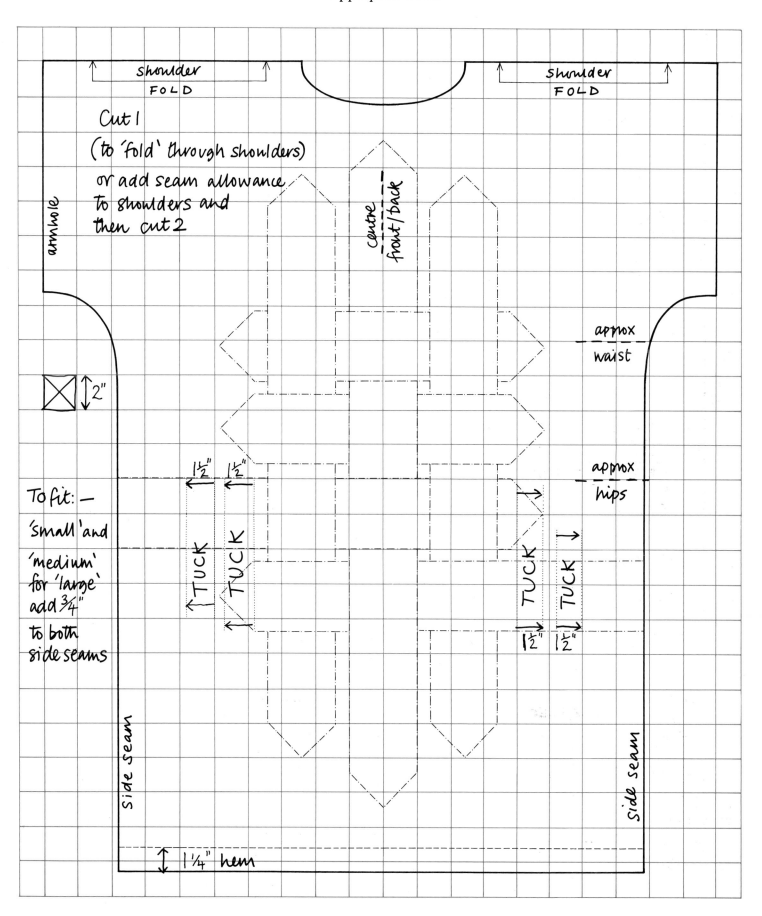

shoulder
FOLD

shoulder
FOLD

armhole

Cut 1

(to 'fold' through shoulders)

or add seam allowance
to shoulders and
then cut 2

centre
front/back

⊠ ↕ 2"

approx
waist

approx
hips

To fit:—
'small' and
'medium'
for 'large'
add ¾"
to both
side seams

1½" 1½"

TUCK TUCK

TUCK TUCK

1½" 1½"

side seam

side seam

↕ 1¼" hem

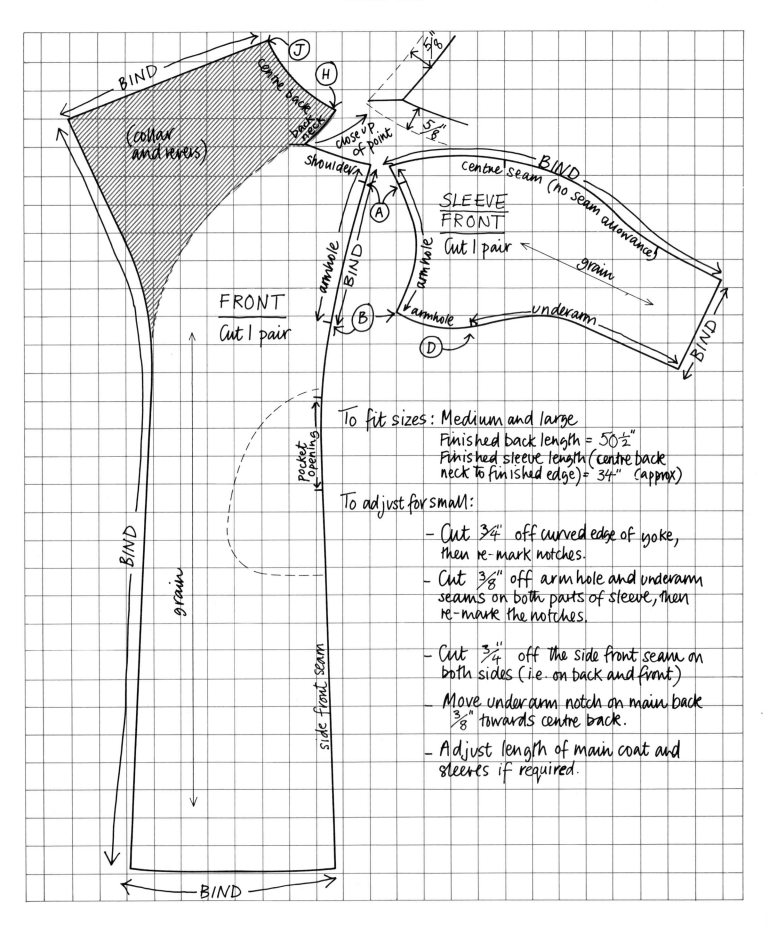

5/8"

5/8"

BIND

(collar and revers)

J

H

centre back

back neck

close up of point

shoulder

A

BIND

FRONT
Cut 1 pair

armhole

BIND

B

armhole

centre seam (no seam allowance)

BIND

SLEEVE
FRONT
Cut 1 pair

grain

armhole

underarm

D

BIND

pocket opening

BIND

grain

side front seam

To fit sizes: Medium and large
Finished back length = 50½"
Finished sleeve length (centre back neck to finished edge) = 34" (approx)

To adjust for small:

- Cut ¾" off curved edge of yoke, then re-mark notches.

- Cut ⅜" off arm hole and underarm seams on both parts of sleeve, then re-mark the notches.

- Cut ¾" off the side front seam on both sides (i.e. on back and front)

- Move underarm notch on main back ⅜" towards centre back.

- Adjust length of main coat and sleeves if required.

BIND

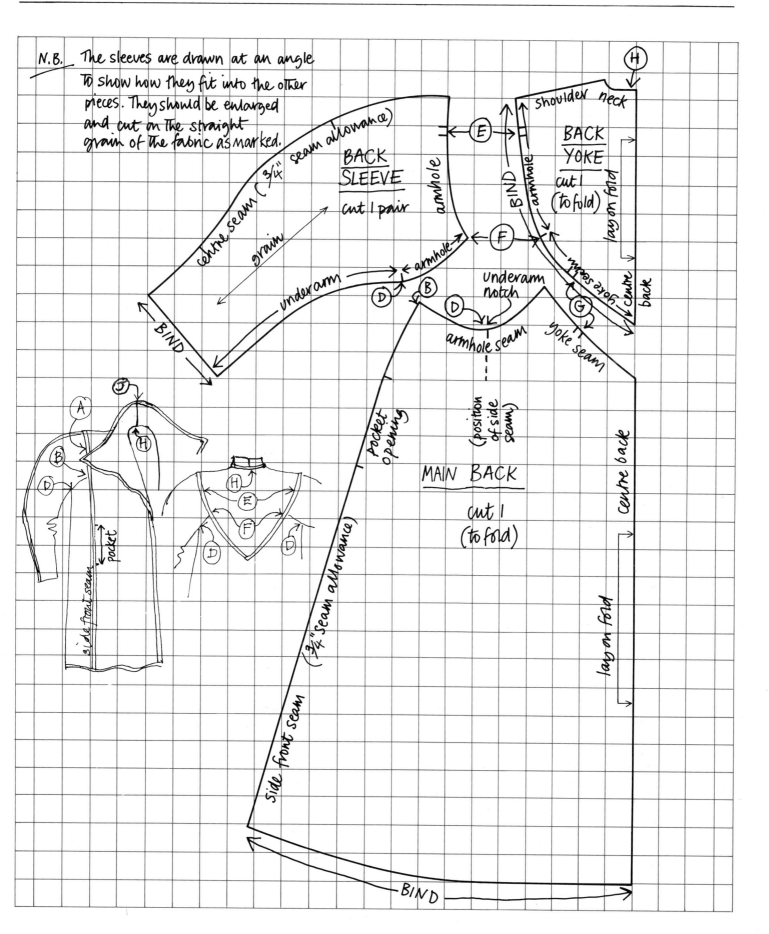

N.B. The sleeves are drawn at an angle to show how they fit into the other pieces. They should be enlarged and cut on the straight grain of the fabric as marked.

BACK SLEEVE
cut 1 pair

centre seam (3/4" seam allowance)

grain

underarm

armhole

BIND

BACK YOKE
cut 1
(to fold)

shoulder neck

BIND

armhole

lay on fold

yoke seam

centre back

underarm notch

armhole seam

yoke seam

MAIN BACK

cut 1
(to fold)

(position of side seam)

pocket opening

side front seam (3/4" seam allowance)

centre back

lay on fold

side front seam

pocket

BIND

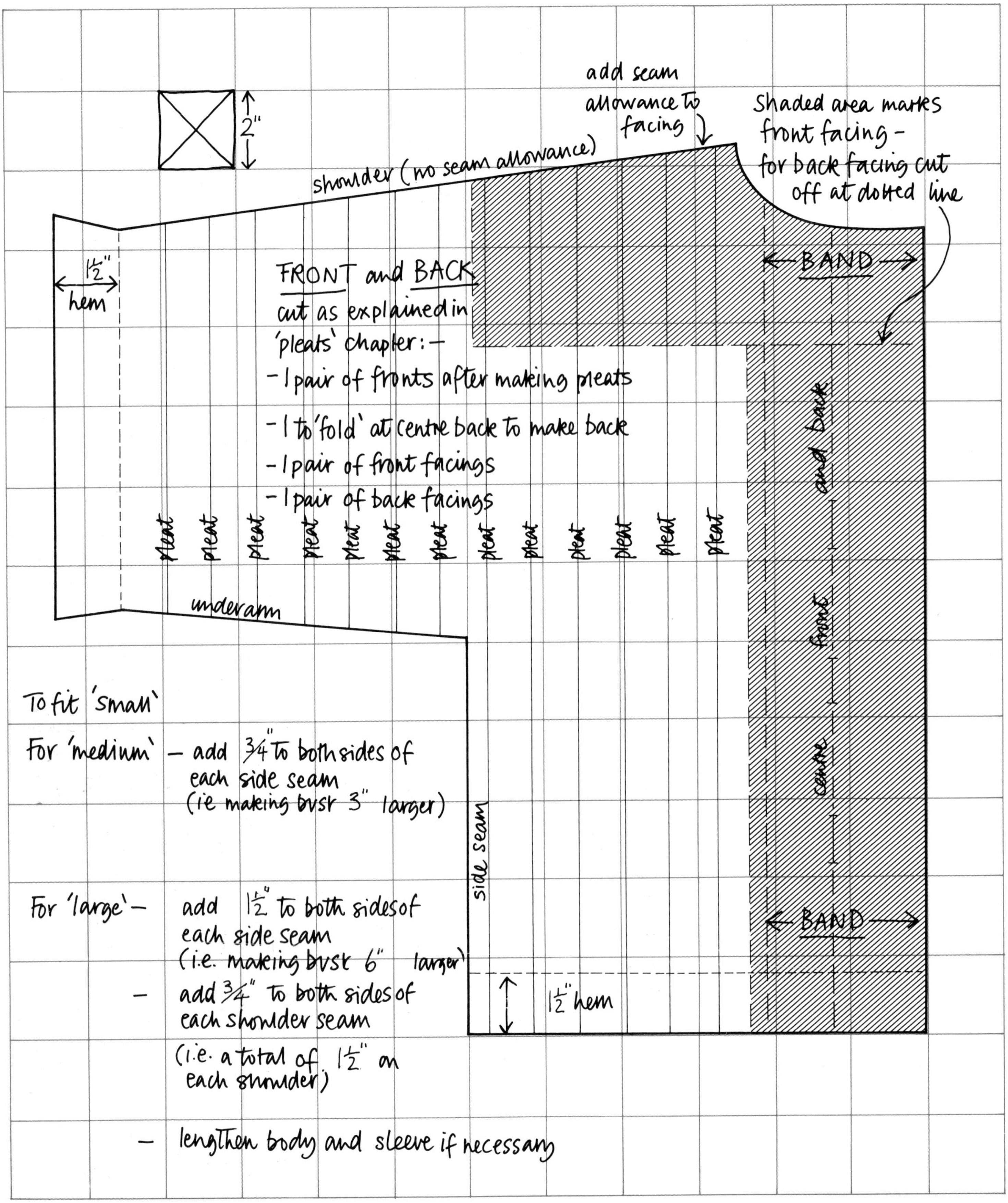

2"

1½"
hem

add seam
allowance to
facing ↓

Shaded area marks
front facing –
for back facing cut
off at dotted line

shoulder (no seam allowance)

←— BAND —→

FRONT and BACK

cut as explained in
'pleats' chapter:—

– 1 pair of fronts after making pleats

– 1 to 'fold' at centre back to make back
– 1 pair of front facings
– 1 pair of back facings

pleat pleat pleat pleat pleat pleat pleat pleat pleat pleat pleat pleat pleat

centre front and back

underarm

side seam

To fit 'small'

For 'medium' – add ¾" to both sides of
each side seam
(i.e. making bust 3" larger)

For 'large' – add 1½" to both sides of
each side seam
(i.e. making bust 6" larger)

– add ¾" to both sides of
each shoulder seam

(i.e. a total of 1½" on
each shoulder)

– lengthen body and sleeve if necessary

←— BAND —→

1½" hem

1½ hem

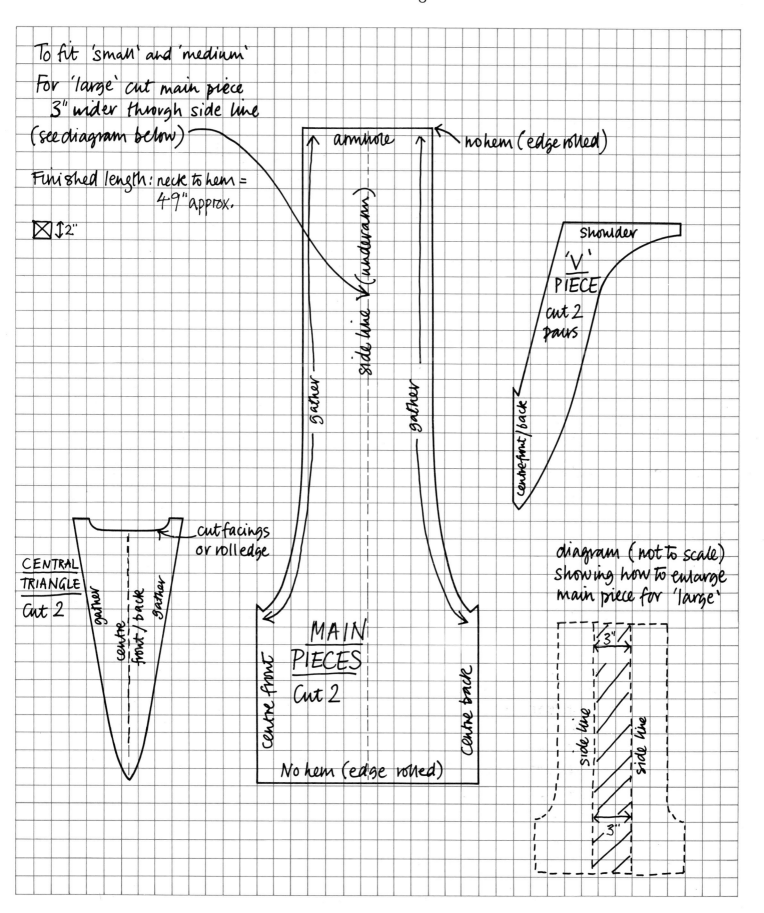

To fit 'small' and 'medium'
For 'large' cut main piece
 3" wider through side line
(see diagram below)

Finished length: neck to hem =
 4·9" approx.

⊠ ↕2"

armhole   no hem (edge rolled)

shoulder

side line ∨ (underarm)

gather   gather

'V'
PIECE
cut 2
pairs

centre front / back

cut facings
or roll edge

CENTRAL
TRIANGLE
Cut 2

gather   centre front / back   gather

diagram (not to scale)
showing how to enlarge
main piece for 'large'

centre front

MAIN
PIECES
Cut 2

centre back

No hem (edge rolled)

3"

side line   side line

3"

Index

Picture credits

Page 12 Top left: Michael Holford
Page 13 Top right: National Portrait Gallery; *below:* Jane Bown
Page 15 Left: The Dryden Collection; *top right and below:* BBC Hulton Picture Library
Page 25 Left: Paul Popper Ltd; *top right:* Paul Tanqueray
Page 27 Left: The Dryden Collection; *top right:* Mary Evans Picture Library
Page 40 Left: Frank Spooner Pictures
Page 43 Left: BBC Hulton Picture Library
Page 51 Left: Paul Popper Ltd; *top right:* The Mansell Collection
Page 53 Transworld Feature Syndicate
Page 65 Transworld Feature Syndicate
Page 67 Left: Paul Popper Ltd; *top right:* The Kobal Collection; *below:* Mary Evans Picture Library
Page 76 Top left: Frank Spooner Pictures
Page 87 Top left and below: Paul Popper Ltd; *right:* Frank Spooner Pictures
Page 101 Left: Mary Evans Picture Library; *top right and below:* BBC Hulton Picture Library
Page 111 Centre: Frank Spooner Pictures
Page 112 Left: Frank Spooner Pictures
Page 123 Left: The Dryden Collection; *top right and below:* BBC Hulton Picture Library
Page 129 Right: BBC Hulton Picture Library
Page 137 The Dryden Collection

All other pictures courtesy of the author and her friends.

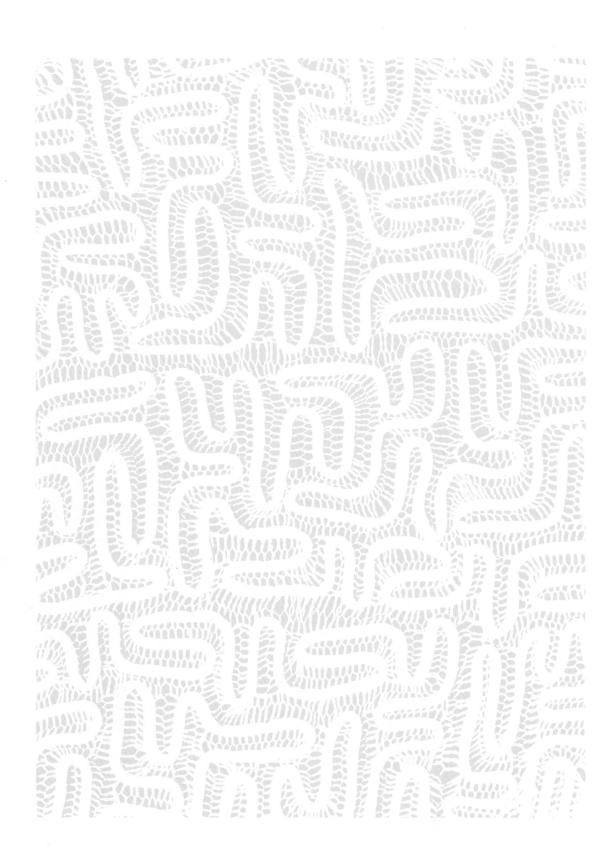

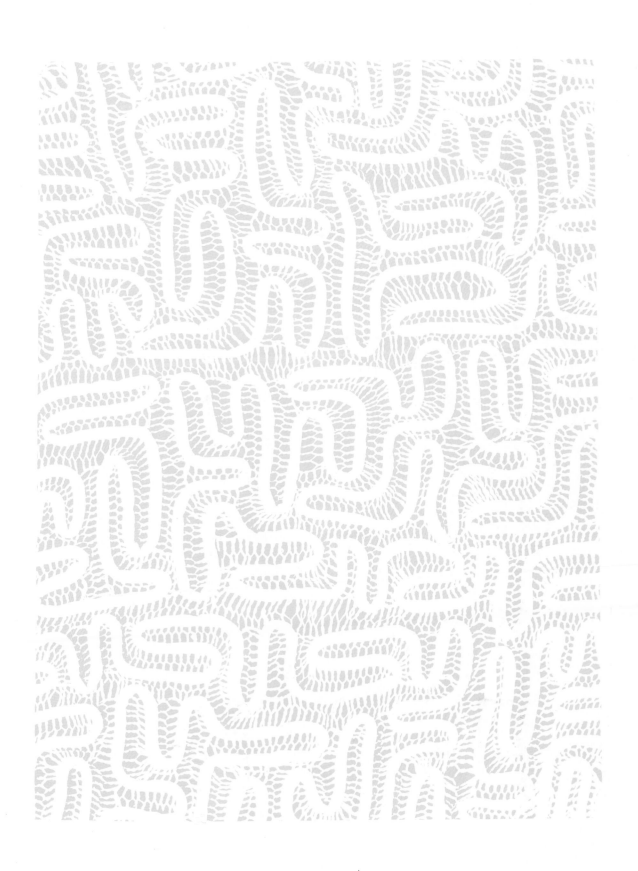

DEC - 1985